UNDERSTANDING ARTIFICIAL INTELLIGENCE {AI}

A COMPREHENSIVE BEGINNERS GUIDE TO THE WORLD OF ARTIFICIAL INTELLIGENCE

— VOLUME ONE —

J.F. GRALEY

Books of Understanding
Produced by J.F. Graley

CONTENTS

Disclaimer Notice:

This book was developed with the assistance of artificial intelligence (AI) tools. The authors used various AI-powered platforms and applications, including but not limited to Grammarly Premium and ChatGPT, to enhance the writing, editing, and content creation processes. While these tools provide valuable support in ensuring the clarity, accuracy, and comprehensiveness of the information presented, the responsibility for the content and opinions expressed in this book lies solely with the authors.

Please note that the information contained within this book has been derived from various sources and is intended for educational and entertainment purposes only. Every effort has been made to present accurate, up-to-date, reliable, and complete information, but no warranties of any kind are declared or implied.

By reading this book, the reader agrees that the Author(s) and Publisher(s) are under no circumstances responsible for any direct or indirect losses incurred from using the information contained within this book, including, but not limited to, errors, omissions, or inaccuracies.

First Print Edition: 09/25/2024

ISBN: 979-8-218-98150-1

Books of Understanding™
contactus@booksofunderstanding.com

For the champions of intellectual curiosity and lifelong learning, this book is dedicated to you. With each chapter, may you find new opportunities to expand your horizons, challenge your assumptions, and grow as a thinker and as a person. Your dedication to the pursuit of knowledge inspires us all. May this book enrich your mind and nourish your spirit on your journey toward greater understanding and comprehension.

—J.F. Graley

ABOUT THE BOOK

Welcome to the first installment of an epic journey into the heart of artificial intelligence. Understanding Artificial Intelligence {AI}: A Comprehensive Beginners Guide to the World of Artificial Intelligence, Volume One is your definitive introduction to the fascinating and rapidly evolving field of AI.

As the first book in a series dedicated to unraveling the complexities of AI, this volume sets the foundation for a deeper exploration of the technology that is transforming our world. Designed for readers with varying levels of knowledge, this book demystifies complex concepts and presents them in an accessible and engaging manner. Whether you are a curious beginner, a student, or a professional looking to dive into AI, this book will provide you with a solid foundation and a comprehensive understanding of AI's principles, history, and future prospects.

The journey begins with an insightful introduction to AI, defining what artificial intelligence truly means and exploring its scope and significance. The book traces the rich history of AI, from its early conceptualizations and key milestones to the contributions of pioneering figures like Alan Turing, John McCarthy, and Marvin Minsky. These historical insights provide valuable context for appreciating the current state of AI and its potential future developments.

Diving deeper, the book explains core concepts and terminology essential for understanding AI and machine learning. It breaks down the differences between AI, machine learning, and deep learning, clarifying their unique characteristics and applications. Detailed chapters explore the types of AI, distinguishing between narrow AI, which excels in specific tasks, and the more ambitious goal of general AI, which aims to replicate human intelligence across a broad range of activities.

The book also covers the fundamental building blocks of AI, including algorithms, models, data preprocessing, and the crucial processes of training, testing, and validation. It provides practical insights into how AI systems are developed and evaluated, ensuring readers gain a thorough understanding of the technical aspects of AI.

Real-world applications of AI are highlighted, showcasing its transformative impact on various industries. From healthcare and finance to manufacturing and everyday life, the book illustrates how AI technologies are enhancing productivity, improving quality of life, and driving innovation. Ethical considerations and societal implications are also addressed, emphasizing the importance of responsible AI development and deployment.

By the end of this comprehensive guide, readers will have a solid understanding of what AI is, how it works, and its potential to shape the future. They will be equipped with the knowledge to appreciate AI advancements and their implications for our increasingly digital and interconnected world. As the first volume in a series, it paves the way for deeper dives into the world of AI, preparing readers for subsequent explorations in future volumes.

A Quick Request Before You Begin

Thank you for choosing *Understanding Artificial Intelligence {AI}* as part of your journey into this fascinating, ever-changing technology.

If you find value in what you're about to read, I'd be incredibly grateful if you could share your thoughts in a review on Amazon.

SCAN TO REVIEW BOOK

Your feedback helps me improve and helps others decide if this book is right for them. Your support means the world to me—thank you for being part of this book series.

Let's begin...

INTRODUCTION

Welcome to the first installment of an epic journey into the heart of artificial intelligence. "Understanding Artificial Intelligence (AI) Volume One" is just the beginning of an exhilarating series that will take you deeper into the world of AI than ever before.

Overview of Artificial Intelligence

Artificial intelligence (AI) is a branch of computer science focused on creating systems capable of performing tasks that typically require human intelligence. These tasks include reasoning, learning, problem-solving, perception, and language understanding. The scope of AI encompasses various techniques and approaches, from rule-based systems and symbolic reasoning to machine learning and neural networks. AI aims to build machines that can mimic cognitive functions such as recognizing patterns, making decisions, and understanding natural language.

The history of AI can be traced back to ancient times when myths and legends spoke of artificial beings endowed with intelligence. However, the formal inception of AI as a scientific discipline began in the mid-20th century. A British mathematician, Alan Turing, laid the groundwork for AI with his concept of a thinking machine and the famous Turing Test. The term "artificial intelligence" was coined by John McCarthy in 1956 during the Dartmouth Conference, marking the birth of AI as an academic discipline. Since then, AI has evolved through various phases, including the development of symbolic AI, expert systems, and the advent of machine learning and deep learning.

The importance and impact of AI in modern society are profound and far-reaching. AI technologies are transforming industries, enhancing productivity, and improving the quality of life. In healthcare, AI is revolutionizing diagnostics and treatment planning. In finance, AI systems enhance fraud detection and enable personalized financial advice. AI-powered personal assistants, like Siri and Alexa, are becoming integral parts of our daily lives, making tasks more convenient. Additionally, AI is driving advancements in autonomous vehicles, smart homes, and robotics, reshaping how we live and work. The potential of AI to solve complex problems and create new opportunities underscores its significance in today's world.

Purpose of the Book

This book aims to provide a comprehensive and accessible introduction to the world of artificial intelligence. It is designed for a broad audience that includes individuals with no prior knowledge of AI and those with a basic understanding who wish to deepen their knowledge. Whether you are a student, a professional looking to transition into the AI field, or simply someone curious about the technology shaping our future, this book aims to demystify AI and make it understandable and relevant.

This book is intended to be user-friendly and engaging. It will guide you through the fundamental concepts of AI, explore its history and evolution, and highlight its importance and impact on modern society. Each chapter is structured to build on the previous ones, gradually increasing in complexity while maintaining clarity. Examples and real-world applications are provided to illustrate key points and make the content relatable.

The structure of the book is designed to provide a logical and cohesive journey through the world of AI. It begins with an overview of AI, its definition, history, and significance. The subsequent chapters delve into the core concepts and terminology, the different types of AI, and the foundational principles of machine learning and deep learning. The book then explores various applications of AI across different industries, highlighting how AI is transforming healthcare, finance, manufacturing, and everyday life. The final sections address the ethical, social, and future considerations of AI, including privacy concerns, bias, fairness, and the potential impact of AI on jobs and society.

By the end of this book, you will have a solid understanding of artificial intelligence, how it works, and its potential to shape the future. You will be equipped with the knowledge to appreciate the advancements in AI and the implications of these technologies for our world. This book is your guide to understanding artificial intelligence, its capabilities, and its role in our increasingly digital and interconnected society.

Join us on this captivating journey into the heart of AI, where innovation meets imagination, and the future unfolds before our eyes.

1

WHAT IS ARTIFICIAL INTELLIGENCE?

BASIC CONCEPTS AND DEFINITIONS

Artificial intelligence (AI) is a branch of computer science dedicated to creating systems capable of performing tasks that typically require human intelligence. These tasks include reasoning, learning, problem-solving, perception, and language understanding. AI aims to build machines that can mimic cognitive functions such as recognizing patterns, making decisions, and understanding natural language.

The concept of AI can be traced back to ancient myths and stories about artificial beings endowed with intelligence. However, AI as a scientific field began in earnest in the mid-20th century with the advent of digital computers. John McCarthy coined the term "artificial intelligence" in 1956 during the Dartmouth Conference, which marked the birth of AI as an academic discipline.

AI systems can be categorized based on their capabilities and functionalities. Weak AI, also known as narrow AI, is designed to perform a specific task, such as facial recognition or language translation. These systems operate under limited constraints and do not possess general intelligence. Examples of narrow AI include virtual assistants like Siri and Alexa, which can perform specific tasks like setting reminders and answering questions.

Strong AI, also referred to as artificial general intelligence (AGI), represents a more ambitious goal. AGI systems would possess the ability to understand, learn, and apply knowledge across a wide range of tasks, much like a human being. These systems would exhibit general intelligence, allowing them to adapt to new situations and solve problems without human intervention. While AGI remains a theoretical concept, significant research efforts are directed toward achieving this level of intelligence.

The fundamental building blocks of AI include algorithms, data, and computational power. Algorithms are sets of instructions that guide the AI system in performing tasks. Machine learning, a subset of AI, involves training algorithms on large datasets to recognize patterns and make predictions. Data is crucial for training AI models, as it provides examples for the system to learn. Advances in computational power, particularly the development of powerful processors and cloud computing, have enabled the training of complex AI models on vast amounts of data.

In summary, AI is a multidisciplinary field that seeks to create systems capable of performing tasks that require human-like intelligence. It encompasses various approaches and techniques, from narrow AI systems designed for specific tasks to the ambitious goal of developing general intelligence. Understanding AI's basic concepts and definitions provides a foundation for exploring its applications and implications.

DIFFERENCE BETWEEN AI, MACHINE LEARNING, & DEEP LEARNING

Artificial intelligence (AI), machine learning (ML), and deep learning (DL) are often used interchangeably, but they represent distinct concepts within the field of artificial intelligence. Understanding the differences between these terms is essential for grasping the scope and capabilities of AI technologies.

Artificial intelligence is the broadest term, encompassing any machine or system that can perform tasks that typically require human intelligence. AI includes a wide range of techniques and approaches, from rule-based systems and symbolic reasoning to machine learning and neural networks. AI aims to create machines that can think, learn, and act autonomously.

Machine learning, a subset of AI, focuses on developing algorithms that allow machines to learn from data and improve their performance over time. Instead of being explicitly programmed with specific rules, ML algorithms analyze large datasets to identify patterns and make predictions. For example, a machine learning algorithm can be trained on historical sales data to predict future sales trends. ML is particularly powerful because it enables systems to adapt to new data and refine their predictions without human intervention.

There are several machine learning types, including supervised, unsupervised, and reinforcement learning. In supervised learning, the algorithm is trained on a labeled dataset, meaning that each training example is paired with the correct output. The goal is for the model to learn the mapping from inputs to outputs so that it can predict the output for new, unseen data. On the other hand, unsupervised learning deals with unlabeled data and aims to find hidden patterns or structures within the data. Reinforcement learning involves training an agent to make decisions by rewarding desirable actions and penalizing undesirable ones, making it suitable for tasks with sequential decision-making.

Deep learning is a specialized subset of machine learning that involves training artificial neural networks with many layers (hence the term "deep") to learn representations of data. Neural networks are inspired by the structure and function of the human brain, with interconnected nodes (neurons) that process information in layers. Deep learning has revolutionized AI by achieving state-of-the-art performance in tasks such as image and speech recognition, natural language processing, and game playing.

For example, convolutional neural networks (CNNs), a type of deep learning model, have demonstrated exceptional capabilities in image recognition tasks. These networks can automatically learn to detect features such as edges, textures, and shapes, enabling them to classify images accurately. Recurrent neural networks (RNNs), another type of deep learning model, are designed for sequential data and have been successful in tasks like language translation and speech recognition.

In summary, AI is the overarching field that includes any machine capable of performing intelligent tasks. Machine learning is a subset of AI focused on developing algorithms that learn from data. In contrast, deep learning is a further subset of machine learning that uses multi-layered neural networks to achieve advanced capabilities. Understanding these distinctions helps clarify the scope and applications of different AI technologies.

TYPES OF AI: NARROW AI VS. GENERAL AI

Artificial intelligence can be broadly categorized into two types based on its capabilities: narrow AI (weak AI) and general AI (strong AI). These categories reflect the extent to which AI systems can perform tasks and exhibit intelligence.

Narrow AI refers to AI systems designed and trained to perform specific tasks. These systems are highly specialized and can excel in their designated areas but lack the ability to generalize their knowledge to other tasks. Narrow AI systems are prevalent in today's technology and are integrated into various applications and devices. Examples of narrow AI include virtual assistants like Siri and Alexa, recommendation systems used by streaming services like Netflix, and image recognition software used in medical diagnostics.

Virtual assistants like Siri and Alexa are prime examples of narrow AI. They can understand and respond to voice commands, set reminders, answer questions, and control smart home devices. However, their capabilities are limited to the tasks they are programmed to perform. Similarly, recommendation systems on platforms like Netflix and Amazon analyze user preferences and viewing history to suggest movies, shows, or products. These systems excel at making personalized recommendations but cannot perform unrelated tasks.

In the medical field, image recognition software powered by narrow AI can analyze medical images, such as X-rays and MRIs, to detect anomalies and assist in diagnosing conditions. These systems can accurately identify patterns and abnormalities, providing valuable support to healthcare professionals. However, they are limited in their image analysis and cannot generalize their knowledge to other medical tasks.

General AI, on the other hand, represents a more ambitious goal in artificial intelligence. General AI refers to systems that can understand, learn, and apply knowledge across a wide range of tasks, much like a human being. These systems would exhibit general intelligence, allowing them to adapt to new situations and solve problems without human intervention. General AI remains a theoretical concept, and significant research efforts are directed toward achieving this level of intelligence.

The distinction between narrow AI and general AI is crucial for understanding the current state of AI technology and its future potential. While narrow AI systems have made significant advancements and are widely used in various applications, the development of general AI poses greater challenges. Achieving general AI requires advanced algorithms and computational power, a deep understanding of human cognition, and the ability to replicate it in machines.

In summary, narrow AI and general AI represent two different levels of artificial intelligence capabilities. Narrow AI systems are specialized and excel in specific tasks. At the same time, general AI aims to create machines with general intelligence that can perform a wide range of tasks and adapt to new situations. Understanding these distinctions provides a clearer perspective on AI technology's current state and future possibilities.

WHAT YOU LEARNED:

Chapter 1 introduced the basic concepts and definitions of artificial intelligence, highlighting its goal to create systems capable of performing tasks that require human-like intelligence. It discussed the differences between AI, machine learning, and deep learning, emphasizing their unique characteristics and applications. Additionally, the chapter explored the types of AI, distinguishing between narrow AI, which excels in specific tasks, and general AI, which aims to replicate human intelligence across a broad range of activities. This foundational understanding sets the stage for delving deeper into AI's history, core concepts, and applications in subsequent chapters.

2

HISTORY & EVOLUTION OF AI

EARLY BEGINNINGS AND KEY MILESTONES

The journey of AI began long before the term was officially coined. It was rooted in ancient myths and philosophical musings about the nature of intelligence and the possibility of creating artificial beings. These early musings laid the groundwork for what would eventually become one of the most transformative fields in modern science and technology.

Ancient Foundations:

The concept of creating intelligent machines can be traced back to ancient civilizations. In Greek mythology, stories of automatons, such as the bronze giant Talos, who guarded the island of Crete, and the mechanical servant of Hephaestus, the god of fire and metalworking, hint at the desire to build intelligent entities. These myths reflect humanity's long-standing fascination with the idea of artificial beings endowed with human-like capabilities.

Philosophers like Aristotle and Descartes also pondered the nature of intelligence and the potential for artificial beings. Aristotle's work on formal logic laid the foundations for later developments in symbolic reasoning, a core aspect of AI. In his meditations, Descartes considered the possibility of mechanical beings that could imitate human actions, though he ultimately concluded that true intelligence was a divine attribute.

Mathematical and Logical Foundations:

Fast forward to the 17th and 18th centuries, the Age of Enlightenment saw significant advancements in mathematics and logic that would later influence AI. Mathematicians like Blaise Pascal and Gottfried Wilhelm Leibniz developed early mechanical calculators, demonstrating the potential for machines to perform complex calculations. Leibniz's work on binary arithmetic laid the groundwork for digital computing, a critical component of modern AI.

In the 19th century, Charles Babbage conceptualized the Analytical Engine, a mechanical general-purpose computer. Although never completed, the Analytical Engine incorporated elements of modern computers, such as programmable instructions and punched cards. Ada Lovelace, often considered the first computer programmer, recognized the potential of Babbage's machine to perform tasks beyond numerical calculations, envisioning it as a tool for manipulating symbols and creating music or art.

Early 20th Century Developments:

The early 20th century saw further advancements in the theoretical underpinnings of AI. A British mathematician and logician, Alan Turing, made groundbreaking contributions to the field. During World War II, Turing played a crucial role in breaking the German Enigma code, showcasing his exceptional problem-solving abilities. In 1950, Turing published his seminal paper "Computing Machinery and Intelligence," in which he posed the provocative question, "Can machines think?" Turing proposed the now-famous Turing Test as a criterion for determining whether a machine can exhibit intelligent behavior indistinguishable from that of a human.

Turing's work laid the foundation for the formal study of AI and introduced key concepts such as the universal Turing machine, a theoretical model for any computation. His ideas about machine intelligence and his visionary thinking continue to influence AI research to this day.

The Dartmouth Conference and the Birth of AI:

The official birth of AI as a distinct field of study is often traced to the Dartmouth Conference held in the summer of 1956. Organized by John McCarthy, Marvin Minsky, Nathaniel Rochester, and Claude Shannon, the conference brought together leading researchers to explore the potential of creating machines that could simulate human intelligence. It was here that John McCarthy coined the term "Artificial Intelligence."

The participants of the Dartmouth Conference envisioned creating machines that could perform tasks typically associated with human intelligence, such as reasoning, problem-solving, and learning. This vision sparked a wave of enthusiasm and optimism, leading to the development of early AI programs and systems.

The Era of Symbolic AI:

In the late 1950s and 1960s, AI research focused primarily on symbolic AI, also known as "Good Old-Fashioned AI" (GOFAI). Researchers developed programs that used symbolic representations and logical rules to solve problems. One of the notable achievements of this era was the Logic Theorist, a program developed by Allen Newell and Herbert A. Simon in 1956. The Logic Theorist was capable of proving mathematical theorems and is considered one of the first AI programs.

The 1960s also saw the development of the General Problem Solver (GPS), another Newell and Simon program aimed to simulate human problem-solving processes. While GPS demonstrated the potential of AI, it also highlighted the limitations of early AI systems, which struggled with complex and real-world problems.

The Rise of Expert Systems:

As AI research progressed, the 1970s brought about a shift in focus towards more practical applications and the development of expert systems. Expert systems were designed to emulate the decision-making abilities of human experts in specific domains. One of this era's most famous expert systems was MYCIN, developed in the early 1970s to diagnose bacterial infections and recommend treatments. MYCIN's success demonstrated the practical utility of AI and spurred further interest in developing AI applications for various industries.

Despite these early successes, the field of AI experienced periods of stagnation and reduced funding, known as "AI winters." The first AI winter occurred in the mid-1970s when the limitations of AI systems became apparent, and the initial optimism gave way to skepticism. Funding for AI research dwindled, and progress slowed.

Renewed Interest and the Advent of Machine Learning:

The 1980s witnessed a resurgence of interest in AI, driven by advances in machine learning and the development of new algorithms. The introduction of backpropagation, a method for training neural networks, marked a significant milestone in the field. Researchers began exploring neural networks and connectionist models, which mimicked the structure and function of the human brain. This era also saw the rise of artificial neural networks (ANNs), which laid the groundwork for modern deep learning.

The 1990s and 2000s saw significant advancements in AI, driven by the exponential growth of computational power and the availability of large datasets. One of the landmark achievements of this period was IBM's Deep Blue, a chess-playing computer that defeated world champion Garry Kasparov in 1997. This victory demonstrated the potential of AI to solve complex problems and outperform human experts in specific domains.

The Era of Big Data and Deep Learning:

In the 21st century, AI has made remarkable strides thanks to the convergence of big data, powerful computing, and advanced algorithms. The development of deep learning, a subset of machine learning, has revolutionized the field. Deep learning models, such as convolutional neural networks (CNNs) and recurrent neural networks (RNNs), have achieved state-of-the-art performance in tasks like image and speech recognition, natural language processing, and autonomous systems.

The rise of big data has played a crucial role in the success of deep learning. The availability of vast amounts of data has enabled researchers to train more complex models, leading to significant improvements in accuracy and performance. The increase in computational power, driven by advances in hardware such as Graphics Processing Units (GPUs) and Tensor Processing Units (TPUs), has further accelerated the development and deployment of AI systems.

Recent Breakthroughs and the Future of AI:

In recent years, AI has continued to achieve groundbreaking milestones. In 2016, DeepMind's AlphaGo, an AI program based on deep reinforcement learning, defeated the world champion Go player Lee Sedol. Go is a complex board game with an immense number of possible moves, making it a significant challenge for AI. AlphaGo's victory was a major breakthrough, demonstrating the potential of deep learning and reinforcement learning to tackle complex, strategic tasks.

Another significant achievement in AI is the development of OpenAI's GPT-3, a state-of-the-art language model that has demonstrated impressive capabilities in natural language understanding and generation. GPT-3 can generate coherent and contextually relevant text, answer questions, and even write essays. Its performance has highlighted the potential of large-scale language models and transformer architectures in advancing AI.

As AI continues to evolve, researchers are exploring new frontiers such as quantum computing, neuromorphic computing, and explainable AI. Quantum computing promises to solve problems currently intractable for classical computers, potentially revolutionizing fields such as cryptography, optimization, and materials science. Neuromorphic computing aims to develop hardware inspired by the human brain, enabling more efficient and powerful AI systems. Explainable AI seeks to make AI models more transparent and understandable, addressing ethical and societal concerns.

The future of AI is undoubtedly exciting, with the potential to transform industries, improve quality of life, and address some of the world's most pressing challenges.

However, it also requires careful consideration of ethical and societal implications, ensuring that AI is developed and deployed responsibly for the benefit of all.

NOTABLE FIGURES & PIONEERS IN AI

The history of AI is shaped by the contributions of numerous visionaries and pioneers who laid the foundations and pushed the boundaries of what is possible. These individuals, through their groundbreaking work and innovative ideas, have profoundly impacted the development of AI. In this section, we will explore the lives and contributions of some of the most influential figures in the field of AI.

Alan Turing

Often regarded as the father of AI, Alan Turing's contributions to the field are monumental. Born in 1912, Turing was a British mathematician and logician who made significant advancements in the foundations of computer science and artificial intelligence. During World War II, Turing played a crucial role in breaking the

German Enigma code, showcasing his exceptional problem-solving abilities and saving countless lives.

In 1950, Turing published his seminal paper "Computing Machinery and Intelligence," in which he posed the provocative question, "Can machines think?" Turing proposed the now-famous Turing Test as a criterion for determining whether a machine can exhibit intelligent behavior indistinguishable from that of a human. The Turing Test remains a fundamental concept in AI, serving as a benchmark for evaluating machine intelligence.

Turing's work laid the foundation for the formal study of AI and introduced key concepts such as the universal Turing machine, a theoretical model for any computation. His ideas about machine intelligence and his visionary thinking continue to influence AI research to this day. Tragically, Turing's life was cut short in 1954, but his legacy lives on through the continued advancement of AI.

John McCarthy

John McCarthy, born in 1927, is credited with coining the term "Artificial Intelligence" and organizing the Dartmouth Conference in 1956, which marked the birth of AI as a distinct field of study. McCarthy was an American computer scientist and cognitive scientist who made numerous contributions to AI and computer science.

McCarthy's contributions to AI include the development of the Lisp programming language, which became the standard language for AI research for many years. Lisp's unique features, such as its support for symbolic computation and recursion, made it well-suited for AI applications. McCarthy also made significant advancements in the areas of time-sharing systems and symbolic AI, which have had a lasting impact on the field.

Throughout his career, McCarthy was a strong advocate for the potential of AI to improve human life. He envisioned AI systems that could assist with complex tasks, enhance human decision-making, and ultimately contribute to the betterment of society. McCarthy's visionary thinking and pioneering work have left an indelible mark on the history of AI.

Marvin Minsky

Marvin Minsky, a co-founder of the MIT Media Lab, was a pioneer in AI and cognitive science. Born in 1927, Minsky made significant contributions to the development of AI, particularly in the areas of perception, learning, and problem-solving. His research on perceptrons, a type of artificial neural network, laid the foundation for later developments in machine learning.

In 1969, Minsky co-authored the book "Perceptrons" with Seymour Papert, which explored the limitations of early neural networks. While the book highlighted the challenges and constraints of perceptrons, it also inspired future research in the field. Minsky's work on frames, a knowledge representation structure, contributed to the development of AI systems capable of understanding and reasoning about complex information.

Minsky's contributions to AI extended beyond technical advancements. He explored the philosophical implications of machine intelligence and the potential impact of AI on society. Minsky's visionary ideas and innovative research have profoundly influenced the field of AI and continue to inspire researchers today.

Herbert A. Simon

Herbert Simon was a polymath whose work spanned psychology, economics, and computer science. Born in 1916, Simon made significant contributions to AI through his research on decision-making and problem-solving in humans and machines. He was a co-developer of the Logic Theorist and the General Problem Solver, two of the earliest AI programs.

Simon's research focused on understanding human cognition and developing computational models to simulate human problem-solving processes. His work on bounded rationality and satisficing, concepts that describe how humans make decisions with limited information and cognitive resources, earned him the Nobel Prize in Economics in 1978. Simon's interdisciplinary approach and insights into human cognition significantly influenced AI research.

Throughout his career, Simon emphasized the importance of interdisciplinary collaboration in advancing AI. He believed that understanding human intelligence was key to developing intelligent machines. Simon's contributions to AI, cognitive psychology, and economics have left a lasting legacy and continue to shape the field.

Allen Newell

A collaborator with Herbert Simon, Allen Newell made significant contributions to AI through his work on the Logic Theorist and the General Problem Solver. Born in 1927, Newell was an American computer scientist and cognitive psychologist who focused on understanding human problem-solving processes and developing computational models to simulate them.

Newell's research helped establish the foundations of cognitive psychology and AI. He believed that AI systems could be designed to mimic human cognitive processes, enabling them to solve complex problems and perform tasks typically associated with human intelligence. Newell's work on production systems, a type of rule-based AI, demonstrated the potential of AI to model human thought processes.

Throughout his career, Newell emphasized the importance of empirical research and rigorous experimentation in advancing AI. His contributions to AI and cognitive psychology have had a lasting impact on the field and continue to influence contemporary research.

Geoffrey Hinton

Geoffrey Hinton is often referred to as the "Godfather of Deep Learning." Born in 1947, Hinton is a British-Canadian cognitive psychologist and computer scientist whose pioneering work on neural networks and backpropagation algorithms has advanced the field of deep learning.

Hinton's research on deep belief networks and convolutional neural networks (CNNs) has led to significant image and speech recognition breakthroughs. His work on backpropagation, a method for training neural networks, has enabled the development of more accurate and efficient AI models. Hinton's contributions have paved the way for modern AI applications and continue to influence the field.

Throughout his career, Hinton has been a strong advocate for AI's potential to transform various industries and improve quality of life. His visionary research and innovative ideas have made him one of the most influential figures in the history of AI.

Yoshua Bengio

A leading figure in deep learning, Yoshua Bengio's research has focused on neural networks, generative models, and representation learning. Born in 1964, Bengio is a Canadian computer scientist whose work on deep learning architectures and algorithms has significantly advanced the field.

Bengio's research on deep learning has contributed to the development of models that achieve state-of-the-art performance in various AI tasks, such as image recognition, natural language processing, and autonomous systems. He is one of the co-authors of the influential book "Deep Learning," which has become a standard reference for researchers and practitioners in AI.

Throughout his career, Bengio has been a strong advocate for open science and collaboration in AI research. His contributions to deep learning and his commitment to advancing the field have made him one of the most influential figures in AI.

Andrew Ng

Andrew Ng is a prominent AI researcher and educator known for his work on machine learning and online education. Born in 1976, Ng is a Chinese-American computer scientist whose research on deep learning and reinforcement learning has contributed to significant advancements in AI.

Ng co-founded Google Brain, a deep learning research project, and served as Chief Scientist at Baidu, where he led AI research efforts. His online courses on machine learning offered through platforms like Coursera, have educated millions of learners worldwide, making AI accessible to a broader audience.

Throughout his career, Ng has emphasized the importance of practical AI applications and the potential of AI to address global challenges. His contributions to AI research and education have profoundly impacted the field and continue to inspire the next generation of AI researchers.

MAJOR BREAKTHROUGHS & SETBACKS

The history of AI is marked by periods of rapid progress and significant breakthroughs, as well as setbacks and challenges that have shaped the field's development. Understanding these milestones provides insight into the evolution of AI and its current capabilities.

- **Early Breakthroughs**

The 1950s and 1960s saw several groundbreaking developments in AI. The Logic Theorist, developed by Newell and Simon, demonstrated that machines could perform symbolic reasoning and prove mathematical theorems. The General Problem Solver (GPS) extended this approach to more general problem-solving tasks. These early successes showcased the potential of AI and spurred further research.

- **Expert Systems**

The 1970s and 1980s witnessed the rise of expert systems, which aimed to emulate the decision-making abilities of human experts. MYCIN, an expert system for diagnosing bacterial infections, achieved significant success and demonstrated the practical utility of AI in specific domains. Expert systems were widely adopted in healthcare, finance, and manufacturing industries, leading to commercial applications and economic impact.

Despite expert systems' success, the limitations of rule-based AI became apparent. These systems struggled with tasks that required common-sense reasoning and the ability to handle uncertainty and ambiguity. As a result, the initial optimism about AI's potential began to wane, leading to periods of stagnation known as AI winters.

- **AI Winters**

The first AI winter occurred in the mid-1970s when the limitations of early AI systems became apparent. These systems struggled with real-world complexity and lacked the robustness for practical applications. As a result, funding for AI research dwindled, and progress slowed. Researchers faced significant challenges in scaling AI systems and making them more flexible and adaptive.

The second AI winter occurred in the late 1980s and early 1990s, following the overhyped expectations and subsequent failures of expert systems. The limitations of rule-based systems and the lack of scalability led to disillusionment and a decline in funding. AI research faced significant challenges during these periods, and many projects were abandoned or scaled back.

- **Machine Learning and Neural Networks**

The late 1980s and 1990s saw a resurgence of interest in AI, driven by advances in machine learning and the development of new algorithms. The introduction of backpropagation, a method for training neural networks, marked a significant milestone. Researchers began exploring neural networks and connectionist models, which mimicked the structure and function of the human brain. These developments laid the groundwork for modern deep learning.

- **Deep Blue**

One of the landmark achievements in AI was IBM's Deep Blue, a chess-playing computer that defeated world champion Garry Kasparov in 1997. This victory demonstrated the potential of AI to solve complex problems and outperform human experts in specific domains. Deep Blue's success showcased the power of machine learning and heuristic search algorithms, inspiring further research and development.

Deep Blue's victory was a turning point in AI, demonstrating the capabilities of AI systems to handle strategic and tactical reasoning. Its success highlighted the importance of combining domain-specific knowledge with advanced algorithms to achieve high-performance levels.

- **Rise of Deep Learning**

The 21st century has witnessed remarkable advancements in AI, driven by the convergence of big data, powerful computing, and advanced algorithms. The development of deep learning, a subset of machine learning, has revolutionized the field. Deep learning models, such as convolutional neural networks (CNNs) and recurrent neural networks (RNNs), have achieved state-of-the-art performance in tasks like image and speech recognition, natural language processing, and autonomous systems.

The rise of big data has played a crucial role in the success of deep learning. The availability of vast amounts of data has enabled researchers to train more complex models, leading to significant improvements in accuracy and performance. The increase in computational power, driven by advances in hardware such as Graphics Processing Units (GPUs) and Tensor Processing Units (TPUs), has further accelerated the development and deployment of AI systems.

- **AlphaGo**

In 2016, DeepMind's AlphaGo, an AI program based on deep reinforcement learning, defeated the world champion Go player Lee Sedol. Go is a complex board game with an immense number of possible moves, making it a significant challenge for AI. AlphaGo's victory was a major breakthrough, demonstrating the potential of deep learning and reinforcement learning to tackle complex, strategic tasks.

AlphaGo's success was achieved through the combination of deep learning and Monte Carlo tree search, enabling the AI to evaluate and select the best moves in the game. The victory showcased the power of combining different AI techniques to achieve high levels of performance in complex domains.

- **GPT-3**

OpenAI's GPT-3, a state-of-the-art language model, has demonstrated impressive capabilities in natural language understanding and generation. GPT-3 can generate coherent and contextually relevant text, answer questions, and even write essays. Its performance has highlighted the potential of large-scale language models and transformer architectures in advancing AI.

GPT-3's success is attributed to its massive scale, with 175 billion parameters, making it one of the largest language models ever created. The model's ability to generate human-like text and understand context has opened new possibilities for AI applications in content creation, customer support, and education.

- **Challenges and Ethical Considerations**

Despite these breakthroughs, AI continues to face significant challenges and ethical considerations. Ensuring the fairness, transparency, and accountability of AI systems is crucial to prevent biases and discrimination. Addressing the societal impact of AI, such as job displacement and privacy concerns, requires interdisciplinary collaboration and the development of robust ethical frameworks and regulatory policies.

Bias in AI systems has become a major concern, as biased data can lead to discriminatory outcomes. Researchers are working to develop techniques for mitigating bias and ensuring that AI systems are fair and equitable. Transparency in AI models is also important, as understanding how decisions are made can help build trust and accountability.

The societal impact of AI, particularly on employment, is another critical issue. As AI systems become more capable, there is a risk of job displacement in various industries. It is essential to consider strategies for workforce retraining and upskilling to ensure that workers can adapt to the changing job landscape.

- **Future Directions**

The future of AI holds immense promise, with ongoing research focused on advancing general AI, improving the interpretability of AI models, and addressing ethical and societal challenges. Emerging areas such as quantum computing, neuromorphic computing, and explainable AI are poised to drive the next wave of innovations in the field.

Quantum computing holds the promise of solving problems that are currently intractable for classical computers, potentially revolutionizing fields such as cryptography, optimization, and materials science. Neuromorphic computing aims to develop hardware inspired by the human brain, enabling more efficient and powerful AI systems. Explainable AI seeks to make AI models more transparent and understandable, addressing ethical and societal concerns.

The continued advancement of AI will require interdisciplinary collaboration, responsible development, and a focus on ethical considerations. By building on past successes and learning from setbacks, the field of AI can continue to make significant contributions to society and address some of the world's most pressing challenges.

By understanding AI's history and evolution, we gain insight into the challenges and triumphs that have shaped this dynamic field. As we move forward, building on past successes and learning from setbacks will be essential in realizing AI's full potential to transform our world.

WHAT YOU LEARNED

Chapter 2 examined the fascinating history and evolution of artificial intelligence, charting its journey from ancient myths to a modern scientific discipline. It began by exploring early milestones, such as Alan Turing's groundbreaking work on the theoretical foundations of computation and his introduction of the Turing Test in 1950. The chapter highlighted the pivotal Dartmouth Conference in 1956, where John McCarthy coined the term "artificial intelligence," marking the formal inception of AI as an academic field.

The contributions of key figures in AI, including John McCarthy, Marvin Minsky, Herbert A. Simon, Allen Newell, and Geoffrey Hinton, were discussed in detail. Their pioneering work laid the foundation for various AI subfields, from symbolic AI and expert systems to neural networks and deep learning. The chapter also underscored significant breakthroughs, such as the development of the Perceptron, the success of expert systems like MYCIN and DENDRAL in the 1970s and 1980s, and the resurgence of neural networks leading to advancements in machine learning and deep learning.

The chapter also addressed major achievements, including IBM's Deep Blue defeating world chess champion Garry Kasparov in 1997 and Google's AlphaGo triumphing over Go champion Lee Sedol in 2016. These milestones showcased AI's potential to outperform humans in complex tasks and brought significant attention to the field.

The chapter also discussed setbacks and challenges, such as the AI winters of the 1970s and 1980s, which were periods of reduced funding and interest due to unmet expectations. It emphasized the importance of responsibly harnessing AI's full potential responsibly by overcoming these challenges, including ethical concerns like algorithmic bias and data privacy.

Overall, Chapter 2 provided a comprehensive overview of AI's historical context, key contributors, major milestones, and the evolution of technologies that continued to shape the field. This background set the stage for understanding AI's current advancements and future directions.

3

CORE CONCEPTS & TERMINOLOGY

ALGORITHMS AND MODELS

Algorithms and models are at the heart of artificial intelligence (AI) and machine learning (ML). Algorithms are sets of rules or instructions that a computer follows to perform a task or solve a problem. In the context of AI, these tasks often involve learning from data, making predictions, or identifying patterns. A model, on the other hand, is the output of an algorithm applied to a dataset. It represents the learned patterns or relationships within the data and can be used to make predictions on new, unseen data.

Algorithms and models come in various forms, each suited for different tasks. For example, linear regression is a simple algorithm used to predict continuous values. Imagine you have a dataset containing the sizes and prices of houses, and you want to predict the price of a house based on its size. Linear regression finds the best-fit line that represents the relationship between size and price, allowing you to predict the price of a new house based on its size.

Classification algorithms, such as logistic regression and decision trees, are used to predict categorical outcomes. Suppose you have a dataset of emails labeled as "spam" or "not spam." A classification algorithm learns from this data and can then classify new emails as spam or not spam. Logistic regression uses a mathematical function to estimate the probability that an email is spam. At the same time, decision trees split the data into branches based on features like keywords or sender address.

Clustering algorithms like k-means clustering group similar data points together without predefined labels. For example, in market segmentation, a business might use k-means clustering to group customers based on their purchasing behavior. These clusters help the business identify different customer segments and tailor marketing strategies accordingly.

Training a model involves feeding an algorithm with data, allowing it to learn from the data by adjusting its parameters to minimize errors. This training process is iterative, with the algorithm refining its parameters over multiple cycles to improve accuracy. For instance, the model is trained on a labeled dataset in supervised learning, where each input is paired with the correct output. The model learns the mapping from inputs to outputs, enabling it to make accurate predictions on new data.

Evaluating a model's performance is crucial to ensuring its reliability and accuracy. Common evaluation metrics include accuracy, precision, recall, and F1 score for classification tasks and mean squared error (MSE) or root mean squared error (RMSE) for regression tasks. Cross-validation is a technique used to assess a model's generalizability by training it on different subsets of the data and testing it on the remaining data.

In summary, algorithms and models form the foundation of AI and ML, enabling computers to learn from data and make intelligent decisions. Understanding the principles behind these algorithms and how to evaluate their performance is essential for developing robust and reliable AI systems.

DATA, DATASETS, & DATA PREPROCESSING

Data is the lifeblood of AI and ML. Without data, algorithms have nothing to learn from, and models cannot be trained to make predictions or identify patterns. Data can come in various forms, including structured data (such as spreadsheets and databases), unstructured data (such as text, images, and videos), and semi-structured data (such as JSON and XML files).

A dataset is a collection of data points used for training and testing models. In supervised learning, a dataset is typically divided into two parts: the training set and the test set. The training set trains the model, while the test set evaluates its performance. Sometimes, a validation set is also used to fine-tune the model's parameters and prevent overfitting.

Before feeding data into an algorithm, it often needs to be preprocessed to ensure it is clean and suitable for analysis. Data preprocessing involves several steps, including data cleaning, normalization, transformation, and feature engineering. Data cleaning addresses issues such as missing values, duplicates, and errors in the data. For example, if a dataset contains missing values, these can be handled by removing the affected rows or columns or by imputing the missing values using statistical methods.

Normalization is the process of scaling data to a standard range, typically between 0 and 1. This step is important because it ensures that all features contribute equally to the model, preventing features with larger scales from dominating the learning process. For example, normalization ensures that both features are scaled to the same range in a dataset containing features such as age and income, making them equally important to the model.

Data transformation involves converting data into a format suitable for analysis. This step can include encoding categorical variables, creating new features, and aggregating data. For instance, categorical variables (such as gender or occupation) can be encoded using one-hot encoding, creating binary columns for each category. Feature engineering involves creating new features from existing data to improve the model's performance. For example, in a dataset containing date and time information, additional features such as day of the week, month, and hour can be created to provide more context to the model.

Once the data is preprocessed, it is ready to be used for training and testing models. The quality and quantity of data play a critical role in the success of AI and ML projects. High-quality data with relevant and accurate features enables models to learn effectively and make reliable predictions. Conversely, poor-quality data can lead to inaccurate models and unreliable outcomes.

In summary, data, datasets, and data preprocessing are essential components of the ML pipeline. High-quality data, properly cleaned, normalized, and transformed, is crucial for training effective models. Techniques such as one-hot encoding, feature engineering, and normalization play a significant role in preparing data for analysis.

TRAINING, TESTING, & VALIDATION

The process of training, testing, and validating models is fundamental to the development of effective AI and ML systems. Training involves using a dataset to teach an algorithm to recognize patterns and make predictions. Testing evaluates the model's performance on unseen data to ensure it generalizes well. Validation helps fine-tune the model's parameters and prevent overfitting.

Training a model involves feeding it with a training dataset, allowing the algorithm to learn the relationships between inputs and outputs. During training, the model adjusts its parameters to minimize the error between its predictions and the actual outcomes. This process is iterative, with the model refining its parameters over multiple cycles to improve accuracy. The choice of algorithm and the quality of the training data are crucial factors that influence the model's performance.

Once the model is trained, it must be tested on a separate dataset, the test set. The test set contains data that the model has not seen during training, allowing for an unbiased evaluation of its performance. Common metrics used to assess the model's accuracy include accuracy, precision, recall, and F1 score for classification tasks, as well as mean squared error (MSE) or root mean squared error (RMSE) for regression tasks. Testing provides insights into the model's generalization capabilities and helps identify potential issues such as overfitting or underfitting.

Validation is an additional step used to fine-tune the model's parameters and improve its performance. Cross-validation is a common technique used for this purpose. In cross-validation, the dataset is divided into multiple subsets, and the model is trained and tested on different combinations of these subsets. This process helps ensure that the model performs well across different subsets of the data and is not overly dependent on any single portion of the dataset. For example, k-fold cross-validation involves splitting the dataset into k equal parts, training the model on k-1 parts, and testing it on the remaining part. This process is repeated k times, with each part serving as the test set once, and the results are averaged to obtain a robust evaluation of the model's performance.

Hyperparameter tuning is another important aspect of validation. Hyperparameters are parameters that govern the learning process and are set before training begins. Examples include the learning rate, the number of layers in a neural network, and the number of trees in a random forest. Tuning these hyperparameters is essential for optimizing the model's performance. Techniques such as grid search and random search are commonly used for hyperparameter tuning. Grid search involves exhaustively searching through a predefined set of hyperparameters, while random search explores a random subset of hyperparameters. More advanced techniques, such as Bayesian optimization, use probabilistic models to efficiently identify the most promising hyperparameters.

The training, testing, and validation processes are iterative and often require multiple cycles to achieve the desired model performance. Continuous monitoring and evaluation are necessary to ensure that the model remains accurate and reliable over time. This is especially important in dynamic environments where data patterns may change, necessitating regular updates and retraining of the model.

In summary, training, testing, and validation are critical steps in developing effective AI and ML models. Training involves teaching the model to recognize patterns in data, testing and evaluating its performance on unseen data, and validating and fine-tuning its parameters to prevent overfitting and ensure robustness. By understanding and implementing these processes, practitioners can build reliable and accurate models that generalize well to new data and provide valuable insights and predictions.

WHAT YOU LEARNED

Chapter 3 covered the core concepts and terminology essential for understanding AI and ML. Algorithms and models form the foundation of these technologies, enabling computers to learn from data and make intelligent decisions. Various algorithms, such as linear regression, decision trees, and neural networks, are used to build models for different tasks, and evaluating their performance is crucial for ensuring accuracy and reliability.

Data, datasets, and data preprocessing are vital components of the ML pipeline. High-quality data, properly cleaned, normalized, and transformed, is essential for training effective models. Techniques such as one-hot encoding, feature engineering, and normalization play a significant role in preparing data for analysis.

The processes of training, testing, and validation are fundamental to developing robust AI and ML systems. Training involves teaching the model to recognize patterns, testing to evaluate its generalization capabilities, and validating and fine-tuning its parameters to prevent overfitting. Cross-validation and hyperparameter tuning are important techniques for optimizing model performance.

By mastering these core concepts and implementing best practices in data preparation and model evaluation, practitioners can develop reliable and effective AI and ML models that deliver valuable insights and predictions. Understanding these principles is crucial for anyone looking to delve deeper into the field of AI and make meaningful contributions to its advancements.

In conclusion, Chapter 3 provided a comprehensive overview of the essential components of AI and ML, from algorithms and models to data preprocessing and the processes of training, testing, and validation. These foundational concepts form the bedrock upon which more advanced topics in AI are built, and a solid grasp of these basics is vital for success in the field. As AI continues to evolve and permeate various industries, the importance of these core concepts will only grow, making them indispensable knowledge for current and future AI practitioners.

4

INTRODUCTION TO MACHINE LEARNING

DEFINITION AND TYPES OF MACHINE LEARNING

Machine learning (ML) is a subset of artificial intelligence (AI) that focuses on the development of algorithms and statistical models that enable computers to perform tasks without explicit instructions. Instead, these systems learn from data and improve their performance over time. The core idea behind machine learning is to allow computers to learn patterns and make decisions based on data, similar to how humans learn from experience.

Machine learning can be broadly categorized into three main types: supervised learning, unsupervised learning, and reinforcement learning. Each type has distinct characteristics and is suited for different kinds of tasks.

Supervised learning is the most common type of machine learning. In supervised learning, the algorithm is trained on a labeled dataset, which means that each training example is paired with an output label. The goal is for the model to learn the mapping from inputs to outputs so that it can predict the output for new, unseen data. For instance, in a supervised learning task to classify emails as spam or not spam, the model would be trained on a dataset of emails labeled as "spam" or "not spam." Examples of supervised learning algorithms include linear regression, logistic regression, support vector machines (SVM), and neural networks. Supervised learning is widely used in applications such as image recognition, speech recognition, and medical diagnosis.

Unsupervised learning, on the other hand, deals with unlabeled data. The algorithm tries to find hidden patterns or intrinsic structures in the input data without predefined labels. One common application of unsupervised learning is clustering, where the algorithm groups similar data points together. For example, unsupervised learning can be used in customer segmentation to group customers with similar purchasing behaviors. Another application is dimensionality reduction, where the algorithm reduces the number of variables in a dataset while preserving its essential information. Examples of unsupervised learning algorithms include k-means clustering, hierarchical clustering, and principal component analysis (PCA). Unsupervised learning is often used in exploratory data analysis, anomaly detection, and recommendation systems.

Reinforcement learning is a type of machine learning where an agent learns to make decisions by interacting with an environment. The agent receives feedback in the form of rewards or penalties based on its actions and learns to maximize the cumulative reward over time. Reinforcement learning is inspired by behavioral psychology and is particularly suited for tasks where decision-making is sequential and where actions have long-term consequences.

A classic example of reinforcement learning is training a robot to navigate a maze. The robot receives positive rewards for reaching the end of the maze and negative rewards for hitting walls, and it learns to navigate the maze by maximizing its rewards. Reinforcement learning has been successfully applied in various domains, such as game playing (e.g., AlphaGo), robotics, and autonomous vehicles.

SUPERVISED VS. UNSUPERVISED LEARNING

Supervised and unsupervised learning are two fundamental paradigms in machine learning, each with its own strengths and limitations. Understanding the differences between them is crucial for selecting the appropriate approach for a given task.

In supervised learning, the algorithm is provided with labeled training data, which means that each input example is paired with the correct output. The primary goal of supervised learning is to learn a mapping from inputs to outputs so that the model can make accurate predictions on new, unseen data. This process involves minimizing a loss function, which measures the difference between the predicted and actual outputs. Supervised learning is highly effective for tasks where historical data with known outcomes is available. For example, in a supervised learning task to predict house prices, the model would be trained on a dataset containing features such as the size of the house, the number of bedrooms, and the location, along with the corresponding prices. Once trained, the model can predict the price of a new house based on its features.

Supervised learning can be further divided into two main categories: classification and regression. Classification tasks involve predicting discrete labels, such as whether an email is spam or not or whether a tumor is malignant or benign. Regression tasks, on the other hand, involve predicting continuous values, such as predicting the temperature for the next day or estimating a person's weight based on height and age. Common algorithms used in supervised learning include decision trees, random forests, support vector machines (SVM), k-nearest neighbors (k-NN), and neural networks.

Unsupervised learning, in contrast, deals with unlabeled data. The algorithm's goal is to identify patterns, structures, or relationships within the data without the guidance of predefined labels. This makes unsupervised learning particularly useful for exploratory data analysis and situations where labeled data is scarce or expensive to obtain. Clustering is one of the most common tasks in unsupervised learning, where the algorithm groups similar data points together based on their features. For example, clustering can be used in market segmentation to group customers with similar purchasing behaviors, allowing businesses to tailor marketing strategies to different customer segments. Another common task is dimensionality reduction, which involves reducing the number of variables in a dataset while preserving its essential information. Principal component analysis (PCA) and t-distributed stochastic neighbor embedding (t-SNE) are popular dimensionality reduction techniques used to visualize high-dimensional data and identify underlying structures.

Unsupervised learning is also valuable for anomaly detection, where the goal is to identify unusual or rare events in the data. For instance, in network security, unsupervised learning can be used to detect abnormal patterns of network traffic that may indicate a cyber attack. In manufacturing, it can be used to identify defective products on an assembly line.

While supervised learning is generally more accurate for predictive tasks due to the availability of labeled data, unsupervised learning provides greater flexibility for exploring and understanding complex datasets. The choice between supervised and unsupervised learning depends on the specific problem, the nature of the data, and the availability of labeled examples.

KEY ALGORITHMS & TECHNIQUES

Machine learning encompasses a wide range of algorithms and techniques, each suited to different types of tasks and data. Understanding these key algorithms is essential for building effective machine-learning models.

One of the simplest and most intuitive algorithms in supervised learning is linear regression. Linear regression models the relationship between a dependent variable and one or more independent variables by fitting a linear equation to the observed data. It is commonly used for predicting continuous values, such as sales, prices, and temperatures. Despite its simplicity, linear regression can be quite powerful, especially when the relationship between variables is approximately linear.

Logistic regression, another fundamental algorithm, is used for binary classification tasks. It models the probability of a binary outcome (e.g., yes/no, spam/not spam) using a logistic function. Logistic regression is widely used in applications such as medical diagnosis, fraud detection, and marketing response prediction.

Decision trees are versatile algorithms that can be used for both classification and regression tasks. A decision tree splits the data into subsets based on feature values, creating a tree-like model of decisions. Each node represents a decision point, and each branch represents an outcome. Decision trees are easy to interpret and visualize, making them useful for understanding the decision-making process. However, they can be prone to overfitting, especially with complex datasets.

Random forests are an ensemble learning technique that combines multiple decision trees to improve accuracy and robustness. By averaging the predictions of multiple trees, random forests reduce the risk of overfitting and provide more reliable predictions. Random forests are widely used in various applications, including credit scoring, image classification, and disease prediction.

Support vector machines (SVM) are powerful algorithms used for classification tasks. SVMs find the optimal hyperplane that separates data points of different classes with the maximum margin. This makes SVMs particularly effective for high-dimensional data and tasks where the classes are well-separated. SVMs are used in applications such as image recognition, text classification, and bioinformatics.

K-nearest neighbors (k-NN) is a simple yet effective algorithm used for both classification and regression tasks. In k-NN, the model makes predictions based on the k-closest data points in the training set. Despite its simplicity, k-NN can achieve high accuracy, especially when the data has a clear structure. However, k-NN can be computationally intensive, especially with large datasets, as it requires calculating the distance between the input and all training examples.

Neural networks, inspired by the human brain, are a class of algorithms used for complex tasks such as image recognition, speech processing, and natural language understanding. Neural networks consist of interconnected layers of neurons, each performing simple computations. These networks are trained using backpropagation, where the model's weights are adjusted to minimize the error between predicted and actual outputs. Deep learning, a subset of machine learning, involves neural networks with many layers (deep neural networks) and has achieved state-of-the-art performance in various tasks.

In addition to these traditional algorithms, some advanced techniques and tools enhance machine learning capabilities. Ensemble learning methods, such as boosting and bagging, combine multiple models to improve performance and reduce overfitting. Feature engineering, the process of creating new features from raw data, can significantly impact model performance by providing more relevant information to the algorithm. Hyperparameter tuning, which involves optimizing the learning process's parameters, can further enhance model accuracy and robustness.

Libraries and frameworks like Scikit-learn, TensorFlow, and PyTorch provide powerful tools for implementing and experimenting with machine learning algorithms. Scikit-learn, for example, offers a wide range of algorithms and utilities for data preprocessing, model selection, and evaluation. TensorFlow and PyTorch are popular deep learning frameworks that enable the development of complex neural networks and support advanced techniques such as transfer learning and reinforcement learning.

Machine learning continues to evolve, with ongoing research and innovation driving new algorithms and techniques. Understanding the key algorithms and their applications is essential for building effective models and leveraging the full potential of machine learning. By mastering these concepts, practitioners can tackle a wide range of problems and contribute to the advancement of AI and its impact on various industries.

WHAT YOU LEARNED

Chapter 4 provided an introduction to machine learning, focusing on the definition and types of machine learning, the distinctions between supervised and unsupervised learning, and key algorithms and techniques used in the field.

Machine learning is a subset of artificial intelligence that enables computers to learn from data and improve their performance over time without being explicitly programmed. It is categorized into three main types: supervised learning, unsupervised learning, and reinforcement learning. Supervised learning uses labeled data to train models that can make predictions or classifications based on new data. Unsupervised learning works with unlabeled data to identify patterns and structures within the data, making it useful for exploratory data analysis and clustering tasks.

Reinforcement learning involves training an agent to make decisions by rewarding desirable actions and penalizing undesirable ones, making it suitable for tasks with sequential decision-making.

Supervised learning involves training a model on a labeled dataset, with the primary goal of learning the mapping from inputs to outputs. It is highly effective for tasks where historical data with known outcomes is available, such as predicting house prices or classifying emails as spam or not spam. Supervised learning can be further divided into classification and regression tasks. Unsupervised learning, on the other hand, deals with unlabeled data and focuses on identifying patterns or structures within the data. Clustering and dimensionality reduction are common tasks in unsupervised learning and are useful for market segmentation, anomaly detection, and data visualization.

Key machine learning algorithms include linear regression, logistic regression, decision trees, random forests, support vector machines (SVM), k-nearest neighbors (k-NN), and neural networks. Each algorithm has its strengths and is suited for different types of tasks. For example, linear regression is used for predicting continuous values, while logistic regression is used for binary classification tasks. Decision trees are versatile and easy to interpret, while random forests improve accuracy by combining multiple decision trees. SVMs are effective for high-dimensional data and well-separated classes, while k-NN is simple and effective for structured data. Neural networks, particularly deep learning models, have achieved state-of-the-art performance in complex tasks such as image recognition and natural language processing.

Advanced techniques and tools, such as ensemble learning, feature engineering, and hyperparameter tuning, further enhance machine learning capabilities. Libraries and frameworks like Scikit-learn, TensorFlow, and PyTorch provide powerful tools for implementing and experimenting with machine learning algorithms. Ensemble learning methods, such as boosting and bagging, combine multiple models to improve performance and reduce overfitting. Feature engineering involves creating new features from raw data to provide more relevant information to the algorithm. Hyperparameter tuning optimizes the parameters that govern the learning process, enhancing model accuracy and robustness.

Machine learning continues to evolve, with ongoing research and innovation driving new algorithms and techniques. Understanding the key algorithms and their applications is essential for building effective models and leveraging the full potential of machine learning. By mastering these concepts, practitioners can tackle a wide range of problems and contribute to the advancement of AI and its impact on various industries.

In summary, Chapter 4 provided a comprehensive introduction to machine learning, covering the fundamental concepts, types of learning, and key algorithms and techniques. This foundational knowledge sets the stage for exploring more advanced topics in AI and understanding the transformative potential of machine learning in various fields.

5

DEEP LEARNING & NEURAL NETWORKS

OVERVIEW OF NEURAL NETWORKS

Deep learning is a subset of machine learning that focuses on neural networks, which are algorithms inspired by the human brain's structure and function. Neural networks consist of layers of interconnected nodes, or neurons, each performing simple computations. These networks are designed to recognize patterns in data, making them ideal for tasks such as image and speech recognition, natural language processing, and more.

The basic unit of a neural network is the neuron, which receives input, processes it, and passes the output to the next layer. Neurons are organized into layers: the input layer, which receives the raw data; one or more hidden layers, which perform computations and extract features; and the output layer, which produces the final prediction or classification. Each connection between neurons has an associated weight, which determines the strength of the signal transmitted. During training, the network adjusts these weights to minimize the error between its predictions and the actual outcomes.

Training a neural network involves a process called backpropagation. In backpropagation, the network makes a prediction based on the input data, calculates the error by comparing the prediction to the actual output, and then propagates this error backward through the network. The weights are adjusted to reduce the error, and this process is repeated iteratively, gradually improving the network's accuracy. Optimizers, such as stochastic gradient descent (SGD) or Adam, are used to update the weights efficiently during training.

Neural networks are particularly powerful because they can learn hierarchical representations of data. In the early layers, the network may learn to recognize simple features, such as edges in an image. As the data passes through successive layers, the network combines these simple features to detect more complex patterns, such as shapes and objects. This hierarchical learning enables neural networks to perform well on a wide range of tasks, even when the input data is high-dimensional and complex.

Deep learning has revolutionized various fields by achieving state-of-the-art performance in tasks that were previously difficult for traditional machine learning algorithms. For example, neural networks have been used to develop advanced image recognition systems, such as Google Photos, which can automatically organize and tag images based on their content. Similarly, speech recognition systems like Apple's Siri and Amazon's Alexa leverage neural networks to understand and process spoken language accurately.

Neural networks have also made significant strides in natural language processing (NLP). AI models like OpenAI's GPT-3 can generate human-like text, perform translation tasks, and even create coherent, contextually relevant responses in conversations. These models are trained on vast amounts of text data, enabling them to understand and generate language with remarkable fluency.

Despite their success, neural networks have some limitations. Training deep networks requires large amounts of labeled data and significant computational resources. Additionally, neural networks can be prone to overfitting, where the model performs well on training data but fails to generalize to new, unseen data. Techniques such as dropout, regularization, and data augmentation are used to mitigate overfitting and improve the network's generalization capabilities. Dropout, for example, randomly sets a fraction of the neurons' outputs to zero during training, preventing the network from becoming overly dependent on any single neuron and thus improving its ability to generalize.

STRUCTURE & FUNCTION OF NEURONS

Understanding the structure and function of neurons in a neural network is crucial for grasping how deep learning models operate. A neuron receives input from other neurons, processes this input using an activation function, and then passes the output to the next layer. The activation function introduces non-linearity into the network, enabling it to learn and represent complex patterns in the data.

Each neuron in the network is associated with a weight and a bias. The weight determines the strength of the connection between neurons, while the bias allows the activation function to shift horizontally. When a neuron receives input, it computes a weighted sum of the inputs and adds the bias. This sum is then passed through the activation function to produce the neuron's output.

Common activation functions include the sigmoid function, which squashes the input to a range between 0 and 1; the hyperbolic tangent (tanh) function, which outputs values between -1 and 1; and the rectified linear unit (ReLU), which outputs the input directly if it is positive and zero otherwise. ReLU has become the most popular activation function in deep learning due to its simplicity and effectiveness in mitigating the vanishing gradient problem, where gradients become too small for effective training.

The structure of a neural network is defined by the arrangement of its layers and the connections between neurons. There are several types of neural network architectures, each suited to different types of tasks. Feedforward neural networks, where the connections between neurons do not form cycles, are the simplest type and are used for tasks like classification and regression. Convolutional neural networks (CNNs), which use convolutional layers to process grid-like data such as images, are widely used in computer vision. Recurrent neural networks (RNNs), which have connections that form directed cycles, are used for sequential data like time series and natural language.

In a feedforward neural network, data flows in one direction, from the input layer through the hidden layers to the output layer. Each layer transforms the input data into increasingly abstract representations. In a CNN, convolutional layers apply filters to the input data to extract local features, such as edges or textures, while pooling layers reduce the spatial dimensions, making the network more efficient and invariant to small translations in the input. In an RNN, the network maintains a hidden state that captures information about previous inputs, allowing it to model temporal dependencies in the data.

Training a neural network involves finding the optimal weights and biases that minimize the error in the training data. This is achieved through an iterative process called gradient descent, where the network's parameters are updated in a direction that reduces the error. The backpropagation algorithm computes the gradient of the error with respect to each parameter, enabling efficient updates.

Neurons in a neural network work together to learn complex representations of the input data. In image recognition, for example, early layers of the network might detect edges and textures, while deeper layers recognize more complex structures like shapes and objects. This hierarchical learning enables neural networks to excel at tasks that require understanding intricate patterns and relationships in the data.

DEEP LEARNING ARCHITECTURES (CNNS, RNNS, GANS)

Deep learning encompasses a variety of architectures designed for different types of data and tasks. Convolutional neural networks (CNNs), recurrent neural networks (RNNs), and generative adversarial networks (GANs) are some of the most prominent architectures, each with unique capabilities and applications.

Convolutional neural networks (CNNs) are specifically designed for processing grid-like data, such as images. CNNs use convolutional layers to scan the input data with filters or kernels, which detect local patterns such as edges, textures, and shapes. These filters are learned during training and are capable of recognizing complex features as the data passes through multiple convolutional layers. Pooling layers, typically max pooling, are used to downsample the data, reducing its dimensionality and making the network more efficient while preserving important features. Fully connected layers at the end of the network combine these features to make predictions. CNNs have been highly successful in various computer vision tasks, such as image classification, object detection, and facial recognition. For instance, the AlexNet architecture, which won the ImageNet competition in 2012, demonstrated the power of deep CNNs in achieving breakthrough performance in image recognition.

Recurrent neural networks (RNNs) are designed for sequential data, such as time series, text, and speech. Unlike feedforward networks, RNNs have connections that form directed cycles, allowing them to maintain a hidden state that captures information about previous inputs. This makes RNNs particularly suited for tasks that involve temporal dependencies. However, traditional RNNs suffer from issues like vanishing and exploding gradients, which can make training difficult for long sequences. To address these issues, more advanced architectures like Long Short-Term Memory (LSTM) networks and Gated Recurrent Units (GRUs) were developed. LSTMs and GRUs use gating mechanisms to control the flow of information, allowing them to capture long-range dependencies more effectively. RNNs and their variants are widely used in natural language processing tasks, such as language modeling, machine translation, and sentiment analysis. For example, Google's Neural

Machine Translation system uses LSTMs to achieve state-of-the-art performance in translating text between languages.

Generative adversarial networks (GANs) are a class of deep learning models used for generating new data samples that resemble a given training dataset. GANs consist of two networks: a generator and a discriminator. The generator creates fake data samples while the discriminator evaluates whether the samples are real or fake. The two networks are trained simultaneously in a process called adversarial training, where the generator aims to produce increasingly realistic samples to fool the discriminator, and the discriminator strives to become better at distinguishing real from fake samples. This adversarial process leads to the generation of high-quality data samples. GANs have been used for various applications, such as generating realistic images, enhancing image resolution, creating art, and synthesizing video game environments. For example, NVIDIA's StyleGAN can generate highly realistic human faces that are indistinguishable from real photos, demonstrating the impressive capabilities of GANs in creating synthetic data.

Each of these deep learning architectures has unique strengths and is suited to different types of tasks. CNNs excel at image-related tasks, RNNs are ideal for sequential data, and GANs are powerful for data generation. By leveraging these architectures, deep learning has achieved remarkable success in a wide range of applications, driving advancements in fields such as computer vision, natural language processing, and generative modeling.

Despite their success, deep learning architectures also present challenges. Training deep networks requires substantial computational resources and large labeled datasets. Additionally, understanding and interpreting the learned representations can be difficult, as deep networks often operate as black boxes. Ongoing research in explainable AI aims to address these challenges by developing methods to make deep learning models more transparent and interpretable.

For instance, techniques like Local Interpretable Model-agnostic Explanations (LIME) and Shapley Additive ExPlanations (SHAP) are being used to provide insights into neural networks' decision-making processes. These methods help identify the most influential features in the model's predictions, making it easier to understand and trust AI systems, especially in critical applications like healthcare and finance.

In summary, deep learning and neural networks have revolutionized various fields by enabling the development of powerful models that can learn complex patterns from data. The hierarchical learning capabilities of neural networks, combined with advanced architectures like CNNs, RNNs, and GANs, have led to significant breakthroughs in tasks such as image recognition, language processing, and data generation. As research continues to advance, the potential applications of deep learning are likely to expand, driving further innovations and transforming industries.

WHAT YOU LEARNED

Chapter 5 explored the foundations and advanced architectures of deep learning and neural networks, highlighting their transformative impact on various fields. Neural networks, inspired by the human brain, consist of interconnected neurons organized into layers, each performing simple computations to recognize patterns in data. Training these networks involves adjusting weights through a process called backpropagation, enabling them to learn from data and improve their predictions.

The structure and function of neurons in a neural network are crucial for understanding how deep learning models operate. Neurons receive input, process it using activation functions, and pass the output to the next layer. Different types of activation functions, such as ReLU, sigmoid, and tanh, introduce non-linearity into the network, enabling it to learn complex patterns.

Deep learning encompasses various architectures designed for different types of data and tasks. Convolutional neural networks (CNNs) are particularly effective for image-related tasks, using convolutional layers to detect local patterns and pooling layers to reduce dimensionality. Recurrent neural networks (RNNs) are designed for sequential data, capturing temporal dependencies with advanced variants like LSTMs and GRUs. Generative adversarial networks (GANs) consist of a generator and discriminator working adversarially to produce realistic data samples, demonstrating their power in data generation tasks.

Despite their success, deep learning architectures present challenges, including the need for substantial computational resources, large labeled datasets, and issues with interpretability. Ongoing research in explainable AI aims to address these challenges, making deep learning models more transparent and interpretable.

Deep learning and neural networks have revolutionized various fields, enabling the development of powerful models capable of learning complex patterns from data. As research continues to advance, the potential applications of deep learning are likely to expand, driving further innovations and transforming industries. By understanding the foundations and advanced architectures of deep learning, we can appreciate its impact and explore its future possibilities.

6

AI IN INDUSTRY & BUSINESS

AI IN HEALTHCARE

Artificial intelligence is revolutionizing the healthcare industry, offering new ways to diagnose, treat, and manage diseases. AI technologies enhance medical research, streamline clinical workflows, and improve patient outcomes through predictive analytics, personalized medicine, and automated diagnostics.

One of the most significant applications of AI in healthcare is in medical imaging. AI-powered systems can analyze medical images, such as X-rays, MRIs, and CT scans, to detect abnormalities and assist in diagnosis. For example, Google's DeepMind developed an AI system that can identify over 50 eye diseases from retinal scans with accuracy comparable to that of expert ophthalmologists. This technology allows for earlier detection and treatment of conditions like diabetic retinopathy and age-related macular degeneration, potentially preventing vision loss in patients. Another example is Aidoc, an AI-powered radiology platform that helps radiologists identify and prioritize critical findings, such as brain hemorrhages and pulmonary embolisms, thereby speeding up diagnosis and treatment.

AI is also transforming the field of oncology. Machine learning algorithms can analyze vast datasets of medical records, genomic information, and clinical trials to identify patterns and predict cancer progression. IBM's Watson for Oncology, for instance, uses AI to recommend personalized treatment plans based on a patient's unique genetic profile and medical history. This approach enhances the precision of cancer treatment, tailoring therapies to the individual characteristics of each patient and improving their chances of recovery. Additionally, Tempus, a technology company specializing in precision medicine, uses AI to analyze clinical and molecular data to provide oncologists with actionable insights for personalized cancer treatment.

In addition to diagnostics and treatment, AI is improving patient care through virtual health assistants. These AI-powered chatbots and mobile applications provide patients with real-time medical advice, appointment scheduling, and medication reminders. For example, the AI chatbot Florence helps patients manage their medications by sending reminders and providing information about prescriptions. Virtual health assistants can also monitor patients' symptoms and alert healthcare providers if intervention is needed, thereby reducing the burden on medical staff and ensuring timely care. Another example is Ada, an AI-powered health app that uses a conversational interface to help users understand their symptoms and guide them to appropriate care.

Predictive analytics is another area where AI is making a significant impact. By analyzing historical data and identifying trends, AI systems can predict outbreaks of diseases, hospital readmission rates, and patient outcomes. For instance, the AI platform developed by BlueDot uses machine learning to analyze global datasets and predict the spread of infectious diseases. This technology was one of the first to identify the emerging threat of COVID-19, providing valuable insights to public health officials and helping to contain the outbreak. Similarly, Johns Hopkins University developed an AI model to predict the spread of COVID-19, which helped inform policy decisions and resource allocation during the pandemic.

Despite the numerous benefits, the integration of AI in healthcare also raises ethical and regulatory challenges. Ensuring the privacy and security of patient data is paramount, as healthcare information is highly sensitive. Regulatory frameworks, such as the Health Insurance Portability and Accountability Act (HIPAA) in the United

States, provide guidelines for data protection, but ongoing vigilance and robust security measures are essential. Additionally, the potential for bias in AI algorithms must be addressed to ensure fair and equitable treatment for all patients. Developing diverse and representative datasets, along with transparent and explainable AI models, is crucial for minimizing bias and ensuring ethical AI deployment in healthcare. For example, the AI model used by Optum for predicting patient needs was found to have racial biases, leading to a reassessment and improvement of the model to ensure equitable care.

AI IN FINANCE

Artificial intelligence has also significantly transformed the finance industry. AI technologies enhance financial services by improving fraud detection, enabling algorithmic trading, and providing personalized financial advice.

Fraud detection is a critical application of AI in finance. Traditional methods of detecting fraudulent activities are often reactive and time-consuming. AI, however, can analyze large volumes of transaction data in real time, identifying unusual patterns and flagging potentially fraudulent activities. For example, Mastercard uses AI to monitor transactions and detect fraud with high accuracy. The AI system evaluates various factors, such as transaction amount, location, and user behavior, to determine the likelihood of fraud, allowing for immediate action to prevent unauthorized transactions. Similarly,

HSBC employs AI to detect money laundering activities by analyzing transaction patterns and identifying suspicious behaviors that warrant further investigation.

Algorithmic trading is another area where AI has made a significant impact. AI-driven trading systems use machine learning algorithms to analyze market data, identify trading opportunities, and execute trades at high speeds. These systems can process vast amounts of information, such as stock prices, trading volumes, and economic indicators, to make informed trading decisions. For instance, hedge funds like Renaissance Technologies use AI algorithms to manage their portfolios and achieve consistently high returns. The ability of AI to analyze market trends and execute trades in milliseconds gives it a significant advantage over human traders, who may be limited by the speed and volume of information they can process. Another example is the use of AI by JP Morgan's LOXM platform, which aims to execute trades at optimal prices by analyzing large datasets and predicting market movements.

AI is also transforming the way financial institutions provide personalized advice to their clients. Robo-advisors, such as Betterment and Wealthfront, use AI algorithms to analyze individual financial goals, risk tolerance, and investment preferences to create customized investment portfolios. These platforms offer automated, low-cost financial advice, making wealth management accessible to a broader audience. Additionally, AI-powered chatbots and virtual assistants help customers with banking services, such as account inquiries, transaction history, and loan applications. For example, Bank of America's virtual assistant, Erica, provides customers with personalized insights, financial tips, and alerts about upcoming bills, enhancing the overall banking experience. Similarly, Wells Fargo uses AI to offer predictive banking, providing customers with insights into their spending habits and helping them manage their finances more effectively.

Despite the benefits, the use of AI in finance also presents challenges and risks. Ensuring the transparency and explainability of AI algorithms is crucial for maintaining trust and regulatory compliance. Financial institutions must implement robust governance frameworks to monitor and validate AI systems, ensuring they operate within legal and ethical boundaries. Additionally, the potential for algorithmic bias and market manipulation must be addressed to prevent unfair practices and protect investors. For example, the flash crash of 2010, caused by automated trading systems, highlighted the need for regulatory oversight and safeguards to prevent such incidents in the future.

AI IN MANUFACTURING

The integration of artificial intelligence has profoundly impacted the manufacturing industry, leading to the advent of smart manufacturing and Industry 4.0. AI technologies enhance production efficiency, quality control, and supply chain management through predictive maintenance, automation, and data analytics.

Predictive maintenance is one of the most significant applications of AI in manufacturing. Traditional maintenance practices are often reactive, addressing equipment failures after they occur, which can lead to costly downtime and repairs. AI-powered predictive maintenance systems, on the other hand, use machine learning algorithms to analyze data from sensors and equipment to predict when maintenance is needed. This approach allows manufacturers to address potential issues before they result in equipment failure, reducing downtime and maintenance costs. For example, General Electric's Predix platform uses AI to monitor industrial machinery, predict maintenance needs, and optimize equipment performance, enhancing overall operational efficiency. Another example is Siemens' MindSphere, an industrial IoT platform that uses AI to analyze data from machines and predict maintenance requirements, thereby improving asset performance and reducing operational disruptions.

Automation is another key application of AI in manufacturing. AI-powered robots and automated systems can perform repetitive and complex tasks with high precision and consistency. These robots are used in various stages of production, from assembly and welding to packaging and quality control. Collaborative robots, or cobots, work alongside human workers, assisting with tasks that require dexterity and adaptability. For instance, Universal Robots' cobots are used in industries ranging from automotive to electronics, performing tasks such as assembling parts, polishing surfaces, and performing inspections. The integration of AI and robotics in manufacturing not only increases productivity but also improves product quality by minimizing human error. Another example is FANUC's use of AI in their robotic arms, which can learn and adapt to new tasks, enhancing flexibility and efficiency in manufacturing processes.

AI also plays a crucial role in supply chain management. AI algorithms can optimize supply chain operations by analyzing data from various sources, such as production schedules, inventory levels, and market demand, reducing costs and improving efficiency. For example, Siemens uses AI to predict demand, manage inventory, and optimize logistics in their supply chain, ensuring timely delivery of products and minimizing excess inventory. AI-powered systems can also detect anomalies and disruptions in the supply chain, allowing manufacturers to respond proactively and maintain smooth operations. Another example is the use of AI by DHL, which employs machine learning algorithms to optimize delivery routes, manage warehouse operations, and predict shipment volumes, thereby improving overall logistics efficiency.

Despite the numerous benefits, the adoption of AI in manufacturing also presents challenges. Ensuring the security and integrity of data collected from sensors and equipment is critical, as cyberattacks can disrupt operations and compromise sensitive information. Additionally, the integration of AI and automation raises concerns about job displacement. While AI technologies create new opportunities for highly skilled workers, there is a need for reskilling and upskilling programs to help workers transition to new roles. Manufacturers must also address ethical considerations, such as ensuring fair labor practices and maintaining a safe working environment. For example, the implementation of AI in the automotive industry has led to concerns about the displacement of assembly line workers, highlighting the need for policies and programs that support workforce transition and skills development.

In conclusion, AI is transforming industries and business sectors, driving innovation and efficiency through advanced technologies. In healthcare, AI enhances diagnostics, treatment, and patient care, offering new solutions for medical challenges. In finance, AI improves fraud detection, trading, and personalized services, revolutionizing how financial institutions operate. In manufacturing, AI optimizes production, maintenance, and supply chain management, leading to smarter and more efficient operations. While the integration of AI presents challenges, addressing these issues through robust governance, ethical practices, and continuous learning will enable industries to harness the full potential of AI and create a more innovative and sustainable future.

WHAT YOU LEARNED

AI is revolutionizing various industries, offering transformative benefits and creating new opportunities for innovation and efficiency. In healthcare, AI technologies are enhancing medical imaging, oncology treatment, virtual health assistants, and predictive analytics, significantly improving patient care and outcomes. Examples such as Google's DeepMind, IBM's Watson for Oncology, and the AI chatbot Florence demonstrate the potential of AI to transform healthcare practices.

In the finance sector, AI is improving fraud detection, algorithmic trading, and personalized financial advice. Institutions like Mastercard and HSBC are using AI to detect fraudulent activities, while hedge funds like Renaissance Technologies and JP Morgan's LOXM platform leverage AI for high-frequency trading. Robo-advisors like Betterment and Wealthfront, along with virtual assistants like Bank of America's Erica, are making wealth management and banking services more accessible and personalized.

The manufacturing industry has embraced AI through predictive maintenance, automation, and supply chain optimization. Platforms like General Electric's Predix, Siemens' MindSphere, and Universal Robots and FANUC's use of collaborative robots highlight how AI is enhancing production efficiency, quality control, and logistics management. AI's role in predictive maintenance, exemplified by GE's Predix and supply chain management, as seen with DHL, further underscores its impact on operational efficiency.

Despite the benefits, the integration of AI across these industries poses challenges, including data security, algorithmic bias, job displacement, and ethical considerations. Ensuring robust data protection measures, transparency in AI systems, and implementing reskilling programs for workers are crucial steps to address these challenges. Ethical AI development, which includes fair labor practices and maintaining safe working environments, is essential for creating a sustainable and inclusive future.

By focusing on these aspects, industries can leverage AI to its fullest potential, driving continuous innovation and fostering a more efficient, equitable, and prosperous society. The future of AI in industry and business is promising, with ongoing advancements expected to further enhance capabilities, improve outcomes, and transform traditional practices. As AI technologies evolve, staying ahead of these changes through proactive adaptation and ethical considerations will be key to ensuring their positive impact on society.

A Moment to Reflect

I hope you're finding *Understanding Artificial Intelligence {AI}* as fascinating to read as it was to create. By now, you've explored some of the incredible ways AI is shaping our world—and there's even more ahead to discover!

SCAN TO REVIEW BOOK

If you're enjoying the book so far, I'd love to hear your thoughts. Consider taking a quick break to leave a review on Amazon. Your feedback helps me but also helps others know how this book has impacted you.

Thank you for your support!

Let's continue...

7

AI IN EVERYDAY LIFE

AI IN PERSONAL ASSISTANTS (ALEXA, SIRI)

Artificial intelligence has made significant strides in enhancing our daily lives, with personal assistants like Amazon's Alexa, Apple's Siri, Google Assistant, and Microsoft's Cortana becoming increasingly integral to our routines. These AI-powered assistants utilize natural language processing (NLP) to understand and respond to user commands, making tasks more convenient and accessible.

Alexa, Siri, Google Assistant, and Cortana are designed to handle a variety of tasks, from setting reminders and sending messages to controlling smart home devices and providing information. By processing spoken language and understanding context, these assistants can perform tasks that previously required manual input. For example, users can ask Alexa to play music, check the weather, or control smart home devices such as lights and thermostats. Siri can send text messages, make phone calls, and provide navigation assistance, while Google Assistant can answer questions, manage schedules, and integrate with other Google services. Although less prevalent in the consumer market, Cortana offers similar functionalities, particularly within Microsoft's ecosystem.

These personal assistants are continually evolving, becoming more intuitive and capable. Machine learning algorithms enable them to learn from user interactions, improving their responses and expanding their capabilities over time. For instance, Siri's suggestions become more personalized based on user behavior, and Alexa's "skills" ecosystem allows third-party developers to create new functionalities, enhancing the assistant's versatility. Google Assistant's integration with Google's suite of services provides a seamless experience, enabling users to manage their digital lives effortlessly.

For example, Alexa can integrate with Amazon's shopping service, allowing users to add items to their shopping lists or place orders directly through voice commands. Siri can access Apple's ecosystem, enabling users to control Apple Music, manage their calendars, and interact with other Apple services. Google Assistant, with its integration into Google's ecosystem, allows users to search the web, get directions via Google Maps, and manage their emails through Gmail.

Despite their convenience, AI personal assistants raise

important privacy and security concerns. These devices constantly listen for activation commands, raising questions about data collection and user consent. While companies assert that recordings are only processed when activation words are detected, there have been instances where these systems have captured conversations unintentionally. Ensuring that user data is protected and that privacy policies are transparent is crucial for maintaining user trust. Companies must implement robust security measures to prevent unauthorized access and misuse of personal data.

For instance, in 2019, it was reported that Amazon employees and contractors were listening to voice recordings captured by Alexa to improve the assistant's performance. This revelation raised concerns about privacy and prompted Amazon to introduce new privacy features, such as the ability to delete voice recordings and review privacy settings. Similarly, Apple faced criticism when it was revealed that contractors were listening to Siri recordings, leading the company to halt the program and introduce an option for users to opt out of audio grading.

The future of AI personal assistants looks promising, with advancements in NLP, contextual understanding, and integration with other technologies. As these assistants become more sophisticated, they will likely handle more complex tasks and provide even greater convenience.

However, it is essential to address privacy and security concerns to ensure that these technologies are used responsibly and ethically.

AI IN SMART HOMES

The concept of smart homes has gained significant traction with the integration of AI, transforming how we interact with our living spaces. AI-powered smart home devices and systems enhance convenience, security, and energy efficiency, making homes more intelligent and responsive to the needs of their occupants.

Smart home ecosystems, such as those powered by Amazon's Alexa, Google Assistant, and Apple's HomeKit, allow users to control various devices and systems through voice commands or mobile apps. These ecosystems integrate with a wide range of smart devices, including lights, thermostats, security cameras, door locks, and appliances. For example, users can control lighting and climate settings, monitor home security, and manage household appliances with ease. AI algorithms enable these systems to learn from user preferences and behaviors, optimizing their performance over time.

One key benefit of AI in smart homes is energy efficiency. Smart thermostats, such as the Nest Learning Thermostat, use AI to learn users' schedules and temperature preferences, adjusting settings automatically to maximize comfort and minimize energy consumption. Smart lighting systems, like Philips Hue, can be programmed to turn off when no one is in the room or adjust brightness based on natural light levels, reducing energy usage. These AI-driven adjustments contribute to lower energy bills and a smaller carbon footprint.

For instance, the Nest Learning Thermostat uses machine learning to create a personalized schedule based on the user's habits. It can detect when the house is empty and adjust the temperature accordingly, leading to significant energy savings. Similarly, smart lighting systems like Philips Hue can be controlled remotely via smartphone apps, allowing users to turn off lights they may have forgotten to switch off, further conserving energy.

Home security is another area where AI has made significant advancements. AI-powered security cameras and doorbells, such as Ring and Arlo, use computer vision to detect and identify potential threats. These systems can differentiate between humans, animals, and inanimate objects, reducing false alarms and enhancing the accuracy of alerts. Additionally, AI algorithms can analyze video feeds to recognize familiar faces and detect unusual activity, providing homeowners with real-time notifications and peace of mind.

For example, the Ring Video Doorbell can alert homeowners and provide a live video feed when someone approaches their door. The system can recognize familiar faces, such as family members, and notify the homeowner of any unknown visitors. Arlo security cameras offer similar features, with AI algorithms that can detect motion and send alerts based on predefined zones and activity types.

AI in smart homes also enhances convenience through automation and integration. Voice-activated assistants can automate routine tasks, such as setting alarms, creating shopping lists, and providing reminders. Integration with other smart devices and services allows for seamless control and management of the home environment. For example, users can create custom routines that adjust lighting, play music, and lock doors with a single command. AI-powered smart speakers, like Amazon Echo and Google Nest Audio, serve as central hubs for controlling smart home systems and accessing information.

For instance, a user can create a "goodnight" routine that turns off all lights, locks the doors, and sets the thermostat to a comfortable temperature with a single voice command. Smart speakers like Amazon Echo and Google Nest Audio can also integrate with music streaming services, allowing users to play their favorite songs or radio stations throughout the house.

Despite the benefits, the proliferation of AI in smart homes raises privacy and security concerns. Smart devices collect and process vast amounts of data, including audio, video, and behavioral information. Ensuring that this data is protected from unauthorized access and misuse is paramount. Manufacturers must implement robust encryption and security protocols to safeguard user data. Additionally, transparency in data collection practices and user consent is crucial for maintaining trust.

For example, in 2020, researchers discovered vulnerabilities in popular smart home devices, such as smart locks and cameras, that could be exploited by hackers to gain unauthorized access. To address these concerns, manufacturers have introduced security features such as two-factor authentication, regular software updates, and user education on best practices for securing smart home devices.

The future of AI in smart homes will likely see further advancements in automation, interoperability, and user experience. As AI algorithms become more sophisticated, smart home systems will become even more intuitive and capable of anticipating user needs. However, addressing privacy and security concerns will remain essential to ensure that these technologies are adopted responsibly and ethically.

AI IN TRANSPORTATION

(SELF-DRIVING CARS)

The advent of AI in transportation, particularly in the development of self-driving cars, represents one of the most transformative advancements in modern technology. Autonomous vehicles (AVs) leverage AI to navigate and operate without human intervention, promising to revolutionize how we travel, reduce traffic accidents, and improve efficiency in transportation systems.

Self-driving cars rely on a combination of sensors, cameras, radar, and lidar to perceive their environment. AI algorithms process this data to identify objects, interpret traffic signals, and make real-time driving decisions. Machine learning models are trained on vast amounts of driving data to recognize patterns and predict the behavior of other road users. Companies like Tesla, Waymo, and Uber are at the forefront of developing autonomous driving technology, conducting extensive testing and refining their systems to ensure safety and reliability.

One of the primary benefits of self-driving cars is the potential to significantly reduce traffic accidents. Human error is a leading cause of accidents, and AI systems can process information faster and more accurately than human drivers. Autonomous vehicles are designed to adhere strictly to traffic laws, maintain safe distances, and react promptly to hazards. For instance, Waymo's autonomous vehicles have logged millions of miles in real-world and simulated environments, demonstrating the potential to navigate complex traffic scenarios safely.

For example, in 2018, a Waymo self-driving minivan was involved in an accident caused by a human driver running a red light. The AI system detected the oncoming vehicle and took evasive action, reducing the severity of the collision and demonstrating its ability to respond to real-world hazards.

Self-driving cars also promise to improve traffic flow and reduce congestion. AI algorithms can optimize routes based on real-time traffic data, avoiding congested areas and minimizing travel time. In addition, autonomous vehicles can communicate with each other and with traffic management systems, enabling coordinated movements that reduce stop-and-go traffic. This level of coordination can lead to more efficient use of road infrastructure and lower fuel consumption.

For instance, Tesla's Autopilot system can analyze traffic patterns and adjust the vehicle's speed and lane position to maintain optimal flow. In 2019, Tesla introduced "Navigate on Autopilot," a feature that allows the car to suggest lane changes and navigate highway interchanges based on real-time traffic conditions, further enhancing efficiency.

The convenience offered by self-driving cars extends beyond safety and efficiency. Autonomous vehicles can provide mobility solutions for individuals who are unable to drive, such as the elderly and disabled. Ride-sharing services, like those envisioned by Uber and Lyft, could become more accessible and affordable with autonomous fleets, reducing the need for car ownership and expanding transportation options. Furthermore, self-driving technology can be applied to commercial vehicles, enhancing logistics and delivery services by enabling 24/7 operations without the limitations of human drivers.

For example, in 2020, Nuro received the first-ever regulatory approval from the U.S. Department of Transportation to deploy a commercial autonomous delivery service. Nuro's small, self-driving vehicles are designed to transport goods and groceries to consumers, demonstrating the potential of autonomous technology to revolutionize last-mile delivery.

However, the widespread adoption of self-driving cars faces several challenges. Ensuring the safety and reliability of autonomous systems in all driving conditions, including adverse weather and complex urban environments, remains a significant hurdle. Extensive testing, validation, and regulatory approval are required to address these challenges and build public trust. Additionally, the transition to autonomous vehicles raises concerns about job displacement for professional drivers and the need for new regulatory frameworks to address liability and ethical considerations.

For instance, in 2018, an Uber self-driving car was involved in a fatal accident in Arizona, raising questions about the readiness of autonomous technology and the regulatory measures needed to ensure safety. This incident highlighted the importance of rigorous testing and regulatory oversight in the deployment of self-driving vehicles.

The development and deployment of self-driving cars must also address cybersecurity risks. Autonomous vehicles are connected systems that rely on data from sensors, communication networks, and cloud services. Protecting these systems from cyberattacks and ensuring data privacy is critical to maintaining safety and trust. Manufacturers and policymakers must collaborate to establish robust cybersecurity standards and protocols.

For example, in 2015, researchers demonstrated the ability

to remotely hack into a Jeep Cherokee's infotainment system, gaining control over critical functions such as steering and braking. This incident underscored the importance of cybersecurity in the design and implementation of autonomous vehicles.

In conclusion, AI in transportation, particularly through self-driving cars, has the potential to transform how we travel, enhance safety, and improve efficiency. As technology continues to advance, addressing safety, regulatory, and cybersecurity challenges will be essential for realizing the full benefits of autonomous vehicles. The future of transportation with AI holds promise for a safer, more efficient, and accessible mobility landscape.

WHAT YOU LEARNED

Chapter 7 explored the integration of AI into everyday life, focusing on personal assistants, smart homes, and transportation. AI-powered personal assistants like Alexa, Siri, and Google Assistant enhance convenience by handling tasks through natural language processing. These assistants are becoming more intuitive and capable but raise privacy and security concerns that must be addressed.

For example, Alexa can integrate with Amazon's shopping service, allowing users to add items to their shopping lists or place orders directly through voice commands. Siri can access Apple's ecosystem, enabling users to control Apple Music, manage their calendars, and interact with other Apple services. Google Assistant, with its integration into Google's ecosystem, allows users to search the web, get directions via Google Maps, and manage their emails through Gmail.

Smart homes leverage AI to improve energy efficiency, security, and convenience. AI-powered devices and systems learn from user behaviors to optimize performance, but the collection and processing of data raise important privacy issues. Ensuring robust security measures and transparent data practices is crucial for maintaining trust.

For instance, the Nest Learning Thermostat uses machine learning to create a personalized schedule based on the user's habits. It can detect when the house is empty and adjust the temperature accordingly, leading to significant energy savings. Similarly, smart lighting systems like Philips Hue can be controlled remotely via smartphone apps, allowing users to turn off lights they may have forgotten to switch off, further conserving energy.

The development of self-driving cars represents a transformative advancement in transportation. Autonomous vehicles promise to reduce traffic accidents, improve traffic flow, and provide mobility solutions for various populations. However, ensuring safety, reliability, and cybersecurity, along with addressing regulatory and ethical considerations, is essential for the widespread adoption of autonomous vehicles.

For example, in 2020, Nuro received the first-ever regulatory approval from the U.S. Department of Transportation to deploy a commercial autonomous delivery service. Nuro's small, self-driving vehicles are designed to transport goods and groceries to consumers, demonstrating the potential of autonomous technology to revolutionize last-mile delivery.

AI continues to shape our daily lives, offering numerous benefits while posing challenges that require careful consideration and responsible implementation. By addressing these challenges, we can harness AI's potential to enhance convenience, safety, and efficiency in everyday life. As AI technology advances, it is essential to ensure that its development and deployment are guided by ethical principles and robust regulatory frameworks, ultimately benefiting society as a whole.

8

ADVANCED AI APPLICATIONS

NATURAL LANGUAGE PROCESSING (NLP)

Natural Language Processing (NLP) is a branch of artificial intelligence that focuses on the interaction between computers and human language. By enabling machines to understand, interpret, and generate human language, NLP has revolutionized various applications, from chatbots to language translation. The complexity of human language, with its nuances, ambiguities, and context dependence, poses significant challenges that NLP aims to address.

One of the key applications of NLP is in machine translation. Tools like Google Translate have made significant strides in translating text from one language to another. These systems use sophisticated algorithms to understand the context and meaning of the source text, producing translations that are not only accurate but also contextually appropriate. However, perfecting machine translation remains a challenge due to the subtleties and idiomatic expressions inherent in human languages.

NLP also plays a crucial role in sentiment analysis, which involves determining the emotional tone behind a piece of text. Businesses use sentiment analysis to gauge public opinion about their products or services by analyzing social media posts, reviews, and feedback. For instance, companies can monitor tweets to understand customer sentiment, allowing them to respond promptly to negative feedback and capitalize on positive sentiments.

Another significant application of NLP is in developing conversational agents, such as chatbots and virtual assistants. These systems can handle customer inquiries, provide information, and perform tasks such as booking appointments or making reservations. Apple's Siri, Amazon's Alexa, and Google's Assistant are prime examples of virtual assistants that leverage NLP to understand and respond to user queries. These assistants use speech recognition to convert spoken language into text, NLP algorithms to interpret the text, and natural language generation to produce human-like responses.

NLP is also transforming the healthcare sector. Electronic Health Records (EHRs) contain vast amounts of unstructured text data that can be challenging to analyze. NLP algorithms can process this data to extract valuable information, such as patient histories, treatment plans, and medical conditions. This information can then be used to improve patient care, streamline clinical workflows, and support medical research. For instance, NLP can identify patterns in patient records that indicate potential health risks, enabling proactive interventions.

Despite its advancements, NLP faces several challenges. Language is inherently ambiguous, and words can have multiple meanings depending on the context. Additionally, languages constantly evolve, with new slang, jargon, and expressions emerging regularly. Addressing these challenges requires continuous improvements in algorithms and models and large, diverse datasets for training.

Recent advancements in NLP, such as the development of transformer models like BERT and GPT-3, have significantly improved the performance of NLP systems. These models use deep learning techniques to understand the context and semantics of language, leading to more accurate and human-like text processing. As NLP technology continues to evolve, it holds the potential to further revolutionize how we interact with machines, making communication more natural and efficient.

COMPUTER VISION

Computer vision is another advanced application of AI, enabling machines to interpret and understand visual information from the world. By mimicking the human visual system, computer vision allows AI systems to recognize objects, track movements, and analyze visual data, leading to applications in various fields, from healthcare to automotive.

In the healthcare industry, computer vision is revolutionizing medical imaging. AI-powered systems can analyze medical images, such as X-rays, MRIs, and CT scans, to detect abnormalities and assist in diagnosis. For instance, computer vision algorithms can identify early signs of diseases like cancer, allowing for timely and accurate diagnoses. These systems can also help radiologists by highlighting areas of concern, reducing the likelihood of oversight, and improving diagnostic accuracy.

In the automotive sector, computer vision is a key component of autonomous driving technology. Self-driving cars rely on computer vision to navigate and understand their environment. Cameras and sensors on the vehicle capture real-time images, which are then processed by AI algorithms to identify objects such as pedestrians, other vehicles, and road signs. This information is used to make driving decisions, ensuring the vehicle can operate safely without human intervention. Companies like Tesla, Waymo, and Uber are at the forefront of developing autonomous vehicles that leverage computer vision for safe and efficient transportation.

Computer vision is also transforming the retail industry. AI-powered systems can analyze in-store video feeds to monitor customer behavior, manage inventory, and enhance security. For example, computer vision can track customer movements and interactions with products, providing retailers with insights into shopping patterns and preferences. This information can be used to optimize store layouts, improve product placements, and tailor marketing strategies. Additionally, computer vision can automate the checkout process by recognizing products and facilitating seamless transactions, as seen in Amazon's cashier-less stores.

In agriculture, computer vision is being used to monitor crop health and optimize farming practices. Drones equipped with cameras can capture images of fields, which are then analyzed by AI algorithms to assess crop conditions, detect pests, and identify areas that need attention. This information enables farmers to make data-driven decisions, improving crop yields and reducing resource usage. For instance, computer vision can detect early signs of crop diseases, allowing for targeted interventions and minimizing the use of pesticides.

Despite its advancements, computer vision faces challenges related to data quality, variability, and context. Visual data can be affected by factors such as lighting conditions, occlusions, and variations in object appearance. Developing robust algorithms that can handle these variations and generalize across different environments is an ongoing challenge. Additionally, ensuring the ethical use of computer vision, particularly in surveillance and privacy-sensitive applications, is crucial.

Recent advancements in computer vision, such as convolutional neural networks (CNNs) and generative adversarial networks (GANs), have significantly improved the ability of AI systems to analyze and interpret visual data. These models have been instrumental in achieving breakthroughs in image recognition, object detection, and image generation. As computer vision technology continues to evolve, it holds the potential to further transform industries and improve our understanding of the visual world.

ROBOTICS & AUTOMATION

Robotics and automation represent some of the most tangible and impactful applications of AI, revolutionizing industries and enhancing productivity. By combining AI with robotics, machines can perform complex tasks with precision, efficiency, and adaptability, leading to significant advancements in manufacturing, healthcare, and service industries.

In manufacturing, robotics and automation are driving the fourth industrial revolution, often referred to as Industry 4.0. Automated robotic systems can perform repetitive tasks such as assembly, welding, and packaging with high accuracy and consistency. This not only improves production efficiency but also reduces the likelihood of errors and enhances product quality. Collaborative robots, or cobots, are designed to work alongside human workers, assisting with tasks that require precision and dexterity. These robots can adapt to changing conditions and learn new tasks, making them versatile tools in modern manufacturing.

Robotics and automation are also transforming the logistics and supply chain industry. Automated guided vehicles (AGVs) and drones are used to transport goods within warehouses and distribution centers, reducing the need for manual labor and increasing operational efficiency. AI-powered systems optimize inventory management, predict demand, and streamline the supply chain, ensuring timely deliveries and reducing costs. For example, Amazon's fulfillment centers use a combination of robotics and AI to manage inventory, pick and pack orders, and handle shipping logistics.

In healthcare, robotics and automation are enhancing surgical procedures, rehabilitation, and patient care. Surgical robots, such as the da Vinci Surgical System, enable minimally invasive surgeries with greater precision and control. These robots assist surgeons by providing a high-definition, 3D view of the surgical site and precise manipulation of surgical instruments. In rehabilitation, robotic exoskeletons assist patients with mobility impairments, helping them regain movement and improve their quality of life. Additionally, automation in healthcare facilities streamlines administrative tasks, such as patient registration and record-keeping, allowing healthcare professionals to focus more on patient care.

The service industry also benefits from robotics and automation. AI-powered robots are being used in hospitality, retail, and customer service to enhance the customer experience. For instance, robots in hotels can assist with check-in, room service, and concierge services, providing personalized and efficient service. In retail, robots can help with inventory management, assist customers with product information, and even handle checkout processes. Customer service chatbots and virtual assistants powered by AI can handle inquiries, provide support, and resolve issues, improving customer satisfaction and operational efficiency.

Despite the numerous benefits, the integration of robotics and automation raises concerns about job displacement and the future of work. As machines take over repetitive and manual tasks, there is a risk of job loss in certain sectors. However, it is important to recognize that robotics and automation also create new job opportunities, particularly in areas such as AI development, robotics engineering, and system maintenance. Reskilling and upskilling the workforce to adapt to these changes are crucial for ensuring a smooth transition to an automated future.

Ethical considerations are also paramount in the development and deployment of robotics and automation. It is essential to ensure that these technologies are used responsibly, with respect for human rights and safety.

Establishing regulatory frameworks and industry standards can help address ethical concerns and promote the safe and ethical use of robotics and automation.

The future of robotics and automation looks promising, with advancements in AI, machine learning, and sensor technology driving further innovations. The development of more sophisticated and versatile robots capable of performing complex tasks in various environments will continue to transform industries and improve efficiency. As we move forward, it is essential to balance technological advancements with ethical considerations and ensure that the benefits of robotics and automation are equitably distributed across society.

WHAT YOU LEARNED

Chapter 8 explored advanced AI applications, focusing on natural language processing (NLP), computer vision, and robotics and automation. NLP enables machines to understand, interpret, and generate human language, revolutionizing applications such as machine translation, sentiment analysis, and conversational agents. Despite its advancements, NLP faces challenges related to language ambiguity and context dependence. Recent developments, such as transformer models, have significantly improved NLP performance.

Computer vision allows AI systems to interpret and understand visual information, leading to applications in healthcare, automotive, retail, and agriculture. AI-powered systems can analyze medical images, enhance autonomous driving, monitor customer behavior in retail, and optimize farming practices. Despite its advancements, computer vision faces challenges related to data quality, variability, and context. Recent innovations in algorithms and models have significantly improved the capabilities of computer vision systems, making them more robust and accurate.

Robotics and automation combine AI with physical machines to perform complex tasks with precision and efficiency. In manufacturing, logistics, healthcare, and the service industry, robots and automated systems are enhancing productivity and transforming traditional workflows. The integration of AI with robotics has led to the development of collaborative robots (cobots) that work alongside humans, automated guided vehicles (AGVs) for logistics, and surgical robots for precision healthcare procedures. While robotics and automation offer numerous benefits, they also raise concerns about job displacement and ethical considerations. Reskilling and upskilling the workforce and establishing regulatory frameworks are essential to address these challenges.

In summary, advanced AI applications in NLP, computer vision, robotics, and automation are transforming various industries and improving efficiency and productivity. Ensuring that these technologies are developed and deployed responsibly, with a focus on ethical considerations and equitable distribution of benefits, is crucial for creating a future where AI enhances human capabilities and contributes positively to society. As AI continues to evolve, ongoing research and innovation will drive further advancements, opening new possibilities and addressing emerging challenges in these fields.

9

ETHICAL & SOCIETAL IMPLICATIONS

AI AND PRIVACY CONCERNS

As artificial intelligence continues to advance and integrate into various aspects of our lives, privacy concerns have become increasingly prominent. AI systems often require vast amounts of data to function effectively, raising questions about how this data is collected, stored, and used.

AI systems rely on large datasets to train models and make accurate predictions. This data can include personal information such as names, addresses, social security numbers, financial details, and even behavioral data like browsing history and purchase patterns. The collection of such sensitive information poses significant privacy risks if not handled properly. One major concern is the lack of transparency in data collection practices. Often, users are not fully aware of what data is being collected, how it is being used, and who has access to it. In many cases, consent is obtained through lengthy and complex privacy policies that users may not fully understand.

The storage of personal data also raises privacy concerns. Data breaches and cyberattacks have become increasingly common, putting individuals' personal information at risk. Ensuring that data is stored securely is crucial to protecting user privacy. Encryption and secure storage practices are essential in safeguarding data. However, not all organizations implement these measures effectively, leaving data vulnerable to unauthorized access. Additionally, the rise of cloud computing has introduced new challenges in data security, as data is often stored on third-party servers that may have different security standards.

Even when data is collected and stored securely, concerns remain about how it is used. AI systems can analyze personal data to make decisions that affect individuals' lives, such as credit scoring, hiring, and targeted advertising. These decisions can have significant consequences, and the lack of transparency in AI decision-making processes can lead to issues of fairness and accountability. Moreover, the use of AI for surveillance and monitoring raises ethical questions. Governments and organizations can use AI-powered systems to track individuals' movements, monitor communications, and analyze behavior. While these technologies can enhance security and efficiency, they also pose risks to civil liberties and personal freedom.

To address privacy concerns, various regulatory frameworks have been established globally. The General Data Protection Regulation (GDPR) in the European Union is one of the most comprehensive data protection laws, providing individuals with greater control over their personal data. GDPR mandates that organizations obtain explicit consent for data collection, implement data protection measures, and notify users in the event of a data breach. In the United States, the California Consumer Privacy Act (CCPA) grants California residents similar rights to control their personal data. These regulations represent important steps toward protecting privacy, but challenges remain in enforcing compliance and addressing the evolving landscape of AI and data use.

As AI continues to evolve, robust privacy protections that balance innovation with individual rights are essential. Future advancements may include stronger encryption methods, improved transparency in data collection and usage, and enhanced regulatory frameworks to address emerging privacy challenges. Ethical considerations should be at the forefront of AI development, ensuring that technologies are designed and implemented with respect for privacy and human rights. Collaborative efforts between governments, organizations, and researchers are necessary to create a secure and ethical AI ecosystem.

BIAS & FAIRNESS IN AI

Bias and fairness are critical issues in the development and deployment of AI systems. AI models can inadvertently perpetuate and amplify existing biases in data, leading to unfair and discriminatory outcomes. Addressing these challenges is essential to ensure that AI technologies are equitable and just.

Bias in AI can originate from various sources. The quality and representativeness of training data play a significant role in shaping AI models. If the data used to train an AI system is biased, the model will likely learn and replicate these biases. For example, if a facial recognition system is trained on a dataset predominantly consisting of images of light-skinned individuals, it may perform poorly on images of darker-skinned individuals. The algorithms used to process and analyze data can introduce biases.

Certain machine learning techniques may favor specific outcomes or groups, leading to biased results. Bias can also be introduced by the developers and engineers who design AI systems. Their assumptions, values, and perspectives can influence the choices made during the development process, resulting in biased models.

The presence of bias in AI can have significant consequences, particularly in high-stakes applications. In criminal justice, AI systems are increasingly used for tasks such as risk assessment and predictive policing. Biased algorithms can disproportionately target minority communities, leading to unfair treatment and reinforcing existing inequalities. In hiring and employment, AI-powered recruitment tools can introduce bias in hiring decisions. For instance, if a system is trained on historical hiring data that reflects gender or racial biases, it may continue to favor certain groups over others, perpetuating discrimination. In healthcare, bias in medical AI systems can result in disparities in diagnosis and treatment. For example, an AI model trained on data from predominantly male patients may not perform as well for female patients, leading to unequal healthcare outcomes.

Addressing bias and ensuring fairness in AI requires a multifaceted approach. Using diverse and representative datasets is crucial to reducing bias in AI models. Ensuring that training data includes a wide range of demographic groups and perspectives can help create more equitable systems. Making AI algorithms transparent and explainable allows stakeholders to understand how decisions are made and identify potential sources of bias. Techniques such as interpretable machine learning and model auditing can enhance transparency. Various techniques can be employed to mitigate bias in AI, including re-sampling training data, adjusting model parameters, and using fairness constraints during the training process. Incorporating ethical considerations into the AI development process is essential. This includes establishing guidelines and frameworks for responsible AI use, promoting diversity in AI teams, and engaging with stakeholders to understand and address potential biases.

Governments and regulatory bodies play a crucial role in ensuring fairness in AI. Policies and regulations can mandate fairness assessments, require transparency in AI systems, and enforce accountability for biased outcomes. Collaboration between policymakers, researchers, and industry leaders is necessary to create a fair and inclusive AI ecosystem.

The ongoing research and development in AI fairness aim to create models that are more robust, unbiased, and equitable. Innovations in algorithm design, bias detection, and mitigation techniques will continue to evolve, contributing to the creation of fairer AI systems. It is essential to maintain a continuous dialogue on the ethical implications of AI and address biases proactively. Ensuring that AI technologies benefit all members of society and do not reinforce existing inequalities is a shared responsibility.

THE FUTURE OF WORK & AI

The integration of artificial intelligence into the workplace is transforming the nature of work, creating new opportunities and posing challenges. AI has the potential to enhance productivity, drive innovation, and improve job satisfaction. However, it also raises concerns about job displacement, skill requirements, and the future of human labor.

AI-driven automation is changing the landscape of work by automating routine and repetitive tasks. This enables employees to focus on more complex and creative activities, enhancing overall productivity. AI can automate tasks such as data entry, scheduling, and customer support. For example, chatbots can handle customer inquiries, freeing up human agents to address more complex issues. AI systems can analyze large volumes of data and provide insights to support decision-making.

This includes predictive analytics for market trends, financial forecasting, and operational optimization.

While AI-driven automation may eliminate certain jobs, it also creates new roles and transforms existing ones. The rise of AI has led to the creation of new job roles, such as AI specialists, data scientists, and machine learning engineers. These roles require specialized skills and expertise in AI technologies. AI is transforming traditional job roles by augmenting human capabilities. For example, in healthcare, AI-powered diagnostic tools assist doctors in making more accurate diagnoses, while in manufacturing, robots work alongside human workers to enhance efficiency.

The shift towards an AI-driven workplace necessitates the development of new skills and continuous learning. Proficiency in AI, machine learning, data science, and programming is increasingly in demand. Educational institutions and training programs are essential in equipping the workforce with these skills. In addition to technical skills, soft skills such as critical thinking, problem-solving, and adaptability are crucial. The ability to work collaboratively with AI systems and leverage their capabilities is essential for future success. The rapid pace of technological advancement requires a commitment to lifelong learning. Workers must continuously update their skills to stay relevant in the evolving job market.

The integration of AI into the workplace presents several

challenges and ethical considerations. The automation of routine tasks can lead to job displacement, particularly in sectors such as manufacturing, retail, and administrative services. Addressing the impact on the workforce and providing support for displaced workers is essential. Ensuring that AI technologies are implemented fairly and do not exacerbate existing inequalities is crucial. This includes addressing biases in AI systems and promoting diversity and inclusion in the workplace. The use of AI to enhance productivity must be balanced with considerations for employee well-being and work-life balance. Ensuring that technology does not lead to increased workloads and stress is important.

The future of AI work will likely involve a harmonious integration of human and machine capabilities. Human-AI collaboration will increase, with AI handling routine and data-intensive tasks while humans focus on creative, strategic, and interpersonal aspects of work. This collaboration can lead to higher productivity and job satisfaction. Continuous investment in reskilling and upskilling the workforce will be crucial. Companies, educational institutions, and governments will need to work together to provide training programs that equip workers with the necessary skills for an AI-driven economy. Policymakers will play a key role in shaping the future of work with AI, including creating regulations that protect workers' rights, ensure fair wages, and promote job security in an automated world.

The future of work with AI will likely see advancements in AI, machine learning, and sensor technology. This will enable the development of more sophisticated and versatile robots capable of performing complex tasks in various environments. Innovations in algorithm design, bias detection, and mitigation techniques will continue to evolve, contributing to the creation of fairer AI systems. Ensuring that AI technologies benefit all members of society and do not reinforce existing inequalities is a shared responsibility. Maintaining a continuous dialogue on the ethical implications of AI and addressing biases proactively will be crucial for creating a fair and inclusive AI-driven future.

WHAT YOU LEARNED

Chapter 9 explored the ethical and societal implications of AI, focusing on three key areas: privacy concerns, bias and fairness, and the future of work. The integration of AI into various aspects of life raises significant privacy issues related to data collection, storage, and usage. Addressing these concerns requires robust regulatory frameworks, ethical considerations, and transparent data practices. The General Data Protection Regulation (GDPR) and the California Consumer Privacy Act (CCPA) are examples of regulations that aim to protect individuals' privacy and provide greater control over personal data. Despite these efforts, challenges remain in enforcing compliance and adapting to the evolving landscape of AI.

Bias and fairness in AI are critical issues, as biased algorithms can lead to discriminatory outcomes. Ensuring that AI systems are fair, transparent, and accountable involves using diverse and representative datasets, making AI algorithms explainable, and employing techniques to mitigate bias. Incorporating ethical considerations into AI development, promoting diversity in AI teams, and engaging with stakeholders are essential steps towards creating equitable AI systems. Governments and regulatory bodies play a crucial role in enforcing fairness in AI through policies and regulations that mandate fairness assessments and accountability.

The future of work with AI presents both opportunities and challenges. AI-driven automation can enhance productivity and create new job roles, but it also poses the risk of job displacement. Preparing the workforce for an AI-driven future requires continuous learning, reskilling, and upskilling. Educational institutions, companies, and governments must work together to provide training programs that equip workers with the necessary skills. Human-AI collaboration will become increasingly important, with AI handling routine tasks and humans focusing on creative and strategic activities. Policymakers must create regulations that protect workers' rights, ensure fair wages, and promote job security in an automated world.

In conclusion, addressing the ethical and societal implications of AI is crucial for harnessing its potential responsibly. Ensuring privacy, fairness, and equitable opportunities in the AI-driven future requires collaborative efforts between governments, industry, academia, and civil society. By understanding and addressing these implications, we can create an AI ecosystem that benefits all members of society and contributes to a more equitable and just world.

10

REGULATORY & LEGAL ASPECTS

CURRENT REGULATIONS AND POLICIES

As artificial intelligence continues to evolve and integrate into various sectors, regulatory frameworks and policies are essential to address the ethical, legal, and social implications of AI technologies. Current regulations aim to ensure the responsible development and deployment of AI while protecting individuals' rights and fostering innovation.

The General Data Protection Regulation (GDPR), implemented by the European Union in 2018, is one of the most comprehensive data protection laws globally. GDPR sets strict guidelines for the collection, storage, and processing of personal data, giving individuals greater control over their information. Key provisions of GDPR include obtaining explicit consent from individuals before collecting and processing their personal data, providing the right to access their data, and the right to be forgotten.

Organizations must also ensure data portability, appoint Data Protection Officers (DPOs) for oversight, and face substantial fines for non-compliance, up to €20 million or 4% of global annual turnover.

In the United States, the California Consumer Privacy Act (CCPA) grants California residents similar rights to control their personal data. Enacted in 2018, CCPA enhances privacy protections and transparency in data handling practices. Key provisions include the right to know what personal data is collected, how it is used, and with whom it is shared, the right to delete personal data, the right to opt-out of the sale of personal data, and protection against discrimination for exercising these rights. The California Attorney General enforces CCPA, with non-compliance resulting in fines and penalties.

The European Commission proposed the Artificial Intelligence Act (AIA) in 2021, aiming to create a regulatory framework for AI that promotes innovation while ensuring safety and fundamental rights. The AIA categorizes AI applications based on their risk levels: unacceptable risk, high risk, limited risk, and minimal risk, with different regulatory requirements for each category. Prohibited AI practices, such as social scoring by governments or exploitative practices targeting vulnerable groups, are banned. High-risk AI systems, such as those used in critical infrastructure, healthcare, and law enforcement, must comply with strict requirements, including risk management, data governance, and transparency. The AIA encourages innovation through regulatory sandboxes, allowing companies to test AI systems in a controlled environment with regulatory oversight.

In the United States, the Federal Trade Commission (FTC) provides guidelines for the use of AI and machine learning to ensure these technologies are deployed fairly and transparently. The FTC emphasizes the importance of preventing unfair or deceptive practices. Key guidelines include transparency in AI use, ensuring fairness by avoiding discriminatory outcomes, maintaining accountability for AI system outcomes, and protecting data security to prevent unauthorized access and misuse.

While existing regulations and policies provide a foundation for governing AI, several challenges remain. Global coordination is necessary to avoid regulatory fragmentation and conflicts. Technological complexity makes it difficult for regulators to keep pace with AI advancements and address emerging risks. Striking a balance between fostering innovation and ensuring safety and ethical standards is essential, as overregulation can stifle innovation, while under-regulation can lead to harmful consequences.

The future of AI regulation will likely involve ongoing refinement and adaptation to address new challenges and opportunities. Enhancing transparency, ensuring fairness and accountability, and promoting international cooperation will be key areas of focus. Collaborative efforts between governments, industry stakeholders, and civil society will be crucial in developing effective and forward-looking AI regulations.

INTELLECTUAL PROPERTY & AI

The rise of artificial intelligence has significant implications for intellectual property (IP) law, particularly in areas such as copyright, patents, and trademarks. As AI systems increasingly contribute to the creation and innovation processes, questions arise about ownership, authorship, and the protection of AI-generated works.

Copyright law traditionally protects original works of authorship, such as literature, music, and art. However, the emergence of AI-generated content challenges the conventional understanding of authorship and originality. One primary question is whether AI-generated works can be granted copyright protection and, if so, who holds the copyright. Since AI systems are not legal entities, they cannot hold copyright themselves. The authorship of AI-generated works typically depends on the degree of human involvement in the creation process. When humans collaborate with AI systems to create works, the resulting content may be eligible for copyright protection, with the human collaborator recognized as the author. For works generated entirely by AI without human intervention, the issue of authorship becomes more complex. Some jurisdictions may recognize the programmer or the entity that owns the AI system as the copyright holder.

Copyright law also requires that works be original and possess a minimum level of creativity. Determining the originality of AI-generated works can be challenging, as AI systems often rely on existing data to generate new content. The extent to which AI-generated works meet the originality requirement varies by jurisdiction and legal interpretation.

AI is driving innovation across various fields, leading to the development of new technologies and inventions. Patent law plays a crucial role in protecting these innovations, but it also faces challenges in the context of AI. For an invention to be patentable, it must meet criteria such as novelty, non-obviousness, and utility. AI-related inventions can include both AI systems themselves and inventions developed using AI. Patents can be granted for AI algorithms, models, and architectures, provided they meet the patentability criteria. However, the abstract nature of software and algorithms can complicate the patent application process. Inventions developed using

AI, such as new materials discovered through machine learning, can also be patentable. The challenge lies in demonstrating the inventive step and the role of AI in the innovation process.

Determining inventorship is another critical issue in patent law. Traditionally, patents are granted to human inventors who contribute to the conception of an invention. When AI systems autonomously generate inventions, the question arises as to whether AI can be considered an inventor. Recent legal cases and policy discussions have addressed the issue of AI inventorship. For example, in the United States, the Patent and Trademark Office (USPTO) and the European Patent Office (EPO) have rejected patent applications naming AI systems as inventors, asserting that inventors must be natural persons. However, ongoing debates and legislative efforts may lead to changes in how inventorship is defined in the future.

AI also impacts trademark law, particularly in the context of branding and consumer interactions. AI-generated content, such as logos and marketing materials, raises questions about trademark protection and infringement. Trademarks protect distinctive signs, symbols, and names used in commerce to identify and distinguish goods and services. AI-generated trademarks must meet the same criteria as human-created trademarks, including distinctiveness and non-confusion. AI can be used to generate content that closely resembles existing trademarks, potentially leading to trademark infringement. Determining whether AI-generated content constitutes fair use or infringement involves assessing factors such as the purpose, nature, and market impact of the content.

The intersection of AI and intellectual property law presents several challenges. The rapidly evolving nature of AI technologies creates legal uncertainties regarding ownership, authorship, and protection of AI-generated works. Existing IP laws may need to be adapted to address the unique characteristics of AI and ensure that legal protections keep pace with technological advancements. Achieving global harmonization of IP laws related to AI is essential to provide consistent protection and enforcement across jurisdictions, involving international cooperation and alignment of legal standards.

The future of intellectual property law in the context of AI will likely involve ongoing adaptation and innovation to address the challenges posed by AI-generated content and inventions. Key areas of focus include clarifying authorship and inventorship, balancing innovation and protection, developing new legal concepts, and promoting ethical AI practices. Ensuring that AI technologies are developed and used ethically, with respect for IP rights, will be crucial in maintaining public trust and fostering sustainable innovation.

INTERNATIONAL PERSPECTIVES ON AI REGULATION

The global nature of AI development and deployment necessitates a coordinated international approach to regulation. Different countries and regions have adopted various strategies and frameworks to address the ethical, legal, and societal implications of AI. Understanding these perspectives can provide valuable insights into the future direction of AI regulation.

The European Union (EU) has been proactive in developing comprehensive regulations for AI. The EU's approach emphasizes ethical AI, transparency, and accountability while promoting innovation and competitiveness. Key initiatives include the General Data Protection Regulation (GDPR), which sets strict standards for data protection and privacy; the proposed Artificial Intelligence Act (AIA), which aims to create a regulatory framework for AI categorizing applications based on their risk levels; and the Ethics Guidelines for Trustworthy AI, developed by the European Commission's High-Level Expert Group on AI, outlining principles for developing and deploying ethical AI.

China has emerged as a global leader in AI development, with significant investments in research, infrastructure, and talent. The Chinese government's approach to AI regulation focuses on promoting innovation, economic growth, and national security. Key initiatives include the Next Generation Artificial Intelligence Development Plan, launched in 2017, which outlines China's strategic vision for AI, aiming to become a global AI leader by 2030; the Ethical Guidelines for New Generation Artificial Intelligence, issued by the Ministry of Science and Technology, emphasizing the ethical use of AI, including respect for privacy, fairness, and transparency; and the Regulation on Internet Information Service Algorithm Recommendation, governing the use of algorithmic recommendation systems to ensure transparency, user rights, and security.

The United States has taken a more decentralized approach to AI regulation, with various federal agencies and state governments developing their own policies and guidelines. The U.S. focuses on promoting innovation, economic competitiveness, and national security. Key initiatives include the American AI Initiative, launched in

2019, which aims to maintain U.S. leadership in AI through investments in research and development, workforce development, and regulatory reform; the National Institute of Standards and Technology (NIST) AI Risk Management Framework, focusing on fairness, transparency, and accountability in AI; and the Federal Trade Commission (FTC) Guidelines, emphasizing the importance of fair and transparent AI use and preventing unfair or deceptive practices.

Japan's approach to AI regulation emphasizes ethical considerations, human-centric AI, and collaboration with international partners. The Japanese government aims to leverage AI to address societal challenges such as aging populations and economic sustainability. Key initiatives in Japan include the Artificial Intelligence Technology Strategy, which outlines the country's vision for AI development, focusing on areas such as healthcare, transportation, and manufacturing. The Social Principles of Human-Centric AI, developed by the Cabinet Office, emphasize the importance of human dignity, privacy, and transparency in AI development and deployment. Additionally, the AI Governance Guidelines issued by the Ministry of Economy, Trade, and Industry (METI) provide a framework for the ethical use of AI, including risk management and accountability.

Achieving a harmonized and effective approach to AI regulation requires international cooperation and collaboration. Various international organizations and forums play a crucial role in fostering dialogue and developing common standards. Key initiatives include the Organisation for Economic Co-operation and Development (OECD) AI Principles, which emphasize inclusive growth, human-centered values, transparency, robustness, and accountability. The G20 AI Principles, endorsed by G20 nations, align with the OECD's guidelines, promoting responsible AI development and international collaboration. The United Nations (UN) has established various initiatives to address the ethical and social implications of AI, including the High-Level Panel on Digital Cooperation and the AI for Good Global Summit.

International perspectives on AI regulation highlight several challenges and future directions. Global harmonization of AI regulations across different countries and regions is challenging due to varying legal systems, cultural values, and economic priorities. However, international cooperation is essential to create consistent and effective regulatory frameworks. Ensuring that AI technologies are developed and deployed ethically is a shared global responsibility, including addressing issues related to bias, fairness, transparency, and accountability. Policymakers must balance the need to promote innovation with the need to protect individuals' rights and ensure safety. Overregulation can stifle innovation, while under-regulation can lead to harmful consequences. As

AI technologies are rapidly evolving, regulatory frameworks must adapt to keep pace with these advancements. Ongoing dialogue and collaboration between governments, industry, and civil society are crucial to address emerging challenges and opportunities.

WHAT YOU LEARNED

Chapter 10 explored the regulatory and legal aspects of AI, focusing on current regulations and policies, intellectual property implications, and international perspectives on AI regulation. Current regulations, such as GDPR, CCPA, and the proposed AIA, aim to ensure the responsible development and deployment of AI while protecting individuals' rights and fostering innovation.

Intellectual property law faces challenges in the context of AI, particularly regarding authorship, ownership, and the protection of AI-generated works and inventions. International perspectives highlight the diverse approaches taken by different countries and regions to address the ethical, legal, and social implications of AI.

Achieving global harmonization, promoting ethical AI development, and balancing innovation with regulation are key challenges and future directions in the regulation of AI.

By understanding these regulatory and legal aspects, readers can appreciate the complexities and importance of developing robust and forward-looking AI policies.

11

THE FUTURE OF AI

EMERGING TRENDS AND TECHNOLOGIES

As artificial intelligence continues to evolve, several emerging trends and technologies are shaping the future landscape of AI. These advancements promise to enhance the capabilities of AI systems, making them more powerful, efficient, and accessible.

- **Explainable AI (XAI)**

Explainable AI (XAI) is becoming increasingly important as AI systems are integrated into more aspects of society. Traditional AI models, particularly deep learning algorithms, are often considered "black boxes" because their decision-making processes are not easily interpretable. XAI seeks to address this issue by developing methods that provide insights into how AI systems arrive at their decisions. The goal is to make AI models more transparent, accountable, and fair.

Transparency in AI is crucial for gaining user trust and ensuring that AI systems are used responsibly. For instance, in healthcare, doctors need to understand how an AI system arrived at a particular diagnosis to make informed decisions about patient care. Similarly, in finance, customers and regulators must know the criteria used by AI to approve loans or detect fraud. XAI helps by providing clear explanations that detail the factors influencing an AI model's decisions.

Accountability is another key aspect of XAI. By making AI systems explainable, developers and users can identify and address any biases or errors in the decision-making process. This is particularly important in high-stakes applications such as criminal justice, where biased AI systems can lead to unfair outcomes. XAI also plays a critical role in compliance with regulations like the General Data Protection Regulation (GDPR), which mandates that individuals have the right to explanation regarding automated decisions affecting them.

Despite its benefits, XAI faces several challenges. One major challenge is balancing the complexity of AI models with the need for interpretability. Highly accurate models like deep neural networks are often less interpretable than simpler models. Researchers are working on techniques to make complex models more understandable without sacrificing performance. Another challenge is standardizing XAI methods to ensure consistency across different applications and industries.

- **AI and Quantum Computing**

Quantum computing holds the potential to revolutionize AI by providing unprecedented computational power. Quantum computers leverage the principles of quantum mechanics to perform complex calculations much faster than classical computers. This capability can significantly enhance AI algorithms, particularly in areas that require extensive computation, such as optimization and simulation.

Quantum computing uses qubits, which can exist in multiple states simultaneously, unlike classical bits that are either 0 or 1. This property, known as superposition, along with quantum entanglement, allows quantum computers to process a vast amount of information simultaneously. Quantum supremacy, the point at which quantum computers can solve problems that are infeasible for classical computers, is a significant milestone that researchers are striving to achieve.

In AI, quantum computing can transform optimization problems. For instance, in logistics, quantum algorithms can optimize delivery routes more efficiently than classical algorithms, saving time and resources. In finance, quantum computing can enhance portfolio optimization by rapidly analyzing large datasets to identify the best investment strategies. Additionally, quantum computing can accelerate drug discovery by simulating molecular interactions at a granular level, leading to faster development of new medications.

However, quantum computing is still in its infancy and faces numerous technical challenges. Developing stable and scalable quantum computers is a significant hurdle, as qubits are highly susceptible to environmental disturbances. Researchers are also exploring ways to integrate quantum computing with classical AI systems to leverage the strengths of both technologies. Moreover, quantum computing raises ethical and security considerations, such as the potential for breaking current cryptographic systems, which necessitates the development of new, quantum-resistant encryption methods.

- **AI for Climate Change and Sustainability**

AI is increasingly being leveraged to address climate change and promote sustainability. AI technologies can analyze large datasets, optimize resource usage, and develop innovative solutions to mitigate environmental impact. Climate modeling, energy efficiency, and sustainable agriculture are key areas where AI is making a significant impact.

Climate modeling is essential for understanding and predicting the effects of climate change. AI algorithms can analyze vast amounts of climate data to improve the accuracy of climate models, helping scientists and policymakers make informed decisions. For example, AI can identify patterns and trends in historical climate data, enhancing predictions about future climate conditions and extreme weather events.

Energy efficiency is another critical area where AI can contribute to sustainability. AI can optimize energy consumption in buildings, industries, and transportation, reducing greenhouse gas emissions. Smart grids use AI to manage and optimize electricity distribution and balance supply and demand while integrating renewable energy sources. In transportation, AI can optimize traffic flow and reduce fuel consumption by providing real-time route recommendations.

Sustainable agriculture is vital for feeding a growing global population while minimizing environmental impact. AI-powered systems can monitor crop health, optimize irrigation, and reduce the use of pesticides, promoting sustainable farming practices. For instance, drones equipped with AI can assess crop conditions and identify areas that need attention, allowing farmers to apply resources more efficiently and reduce waste.

Despite its potential, the use of AI for climate change and sustainability faces challenges. Ensuring access to high-quality environmental data is crucial for training accurate AI models. Scalability is another challenge, as AI solutions need to be implemented on a global scale to effectively address environmental issues. Promoting interdisciplinary collaboration between AI researchers, environmental scientists, policymakers, and industry stakeholders is essential for developing and deploying effective AI solutions for sustainability.

- **AI and the Internet of Things (IoT)**

The convergence of AI and the Internet of Things (IoT) is creating new opportunities for intelligent, interconnected systems. IoT devices generate vast amounts of data, which AI algorithms can analyze to derive insights and drive automation. This integration enhances the functionality of smart homes, healthcare, and industrial automation.

In smart homes, AI-powered IoT devices can automate home management, enhancing comfort, energy efficiency, and security. For example, smart thermostats learn user preferences and adjust temperature settings to optimize energy use. AI-powered security systems can monitor home environments, detect unusual activities, and alert homeowners in real time.

Healthcare is another area where AI and IoT are making a significant impact. Wearable IoT devices can monitor patients' health in real-time, providing early warnings and personalized care. For instance, smartwatches equipped with AI can detect irregular heart rhythms and notify users to seek medical attention. Remote monitoring systems allow healthcare providers to track patients' conditions and intervene when necessary, improving patient outcomes and reducing hospital visits.

In industrial automation, AI and IoT can optimize processes, improving efficiency, safety, and productivity. Predictive maintenance is a key application where AI analyzes data from IoT sensors to predict equipment failures and schedule maintenance, reducing downtime and costs. Smart factories use AI to monitor and control production processes, ensuring quality and efficiency.

However, the integration of AI and IoT faces challenges such as interoperability, data security, and standardization. Ensuring that IoT devices from different manufacturers can communicate and work together seamlessly is crucial for creating cohesive systems. Protecting sensitive data generated by IoT devices from cyber threats is another critical concern. Developing industry standards to guide the integration and deployment of AI and IoT solutions is essential for their widespread adoption.

PREDICTIONS & POTENTIAL IMPACTS

The rapid advancement of AI technologies is expected to have profound impacts across various sectors and aspects of life. Here are some key predictions and potential impacts:

- **Workforce Transformation**

AI is set to transform the workforce by creating new job roles while automating routine tasks. While some jobs may be displaced, new opportunities will arise in AI development, data science, and other tech-driven fields. Continuous learning and upskilling will be essential to adapt to these changes. Workers will need to develop new skills to work alongside AI systems and leverage their capabilities.

The shift towards an AI-driven workforce will also require changes in education and training programs. Educational institutions must adapt their curricula to include AI and data science, ensuring that students are prepared for the future job market. Lifelong learning will become increasingly important, with workers needing to continuously update their skills to stay relevant.

- **Healthcare Revolution**

AI will revolutionize healthcare by enhancing diagnostics, personalized medicine, and patient care. AI-powered tools will assist doctors in making accurate diagnoses, developing tailored treatment plans, and monitoring patient health in real time. For example, AI algorithms can analyze medical images to detect diseases at an early stage, improving treatment outcomes.

Personalized medicine, which tailors treatments to individual patients based on their genetic information and health data, will become more prevalent with AI. AI systems can analyze a patient's genetic profile and predict how they will respond to different treatments, allowing doctors to prescribe the most effective therapies. Remote monitoring and telemedicine, powered by AI and IoT, will improve access to healthcare, especially in remote areas.

- **Smart Cities**

The integration of AI and IoT will drive the development of smart cities, where infrastructure, transportation, and services are optimized for efficiency and sustainability. AI will enhance urban planning, reduce traffic congestion, and improve public safety. For example, AI-powered traffic management systems can analyze real-time data to optimize traffic flow and reduce congestion.

Smart city initiatives will also focus on improving energy efficiency and reducing environmental impact. AI can optimize energy use in buildings and public infrastructure, integrate renewable energy sources, and reduce carbon emissions. Public safety will benefit from AI-powered surveillance systems that can detect and respond to emergencies more effectively.

- **Enhanced Customer Experiences**

AI will transform customer experiences across various industries, from retail to finance. AI-powered chatbots and virtual assistants will provide personalized support, while predictive analytics will enable businesses to anticipate customer needs and preferences. For example, AI can analyze customer data to recommend products and services tailored to individual preferences.

In retail, AI will enhance the shopping experience by providing personalized recommendations and improving inventory management. Virtual shopping assistants can help customers find products and answer questions, while AI-powered logistics systems ensure timely delivery. In finance, AI will improve customer service by providing personalized financial advice and automating routine tasks such as account management.

- **Ethical and Social Challenges**

The widespread adoption of AI will raise ethical and social challenges, such as ensuring fairness, transparency, and accountability in AI systems. Addressing these challenges will require robust regulatory frameworks, ethical guidelines, and public engagement. Ensuring fairness in AI involves developing algorithms that do not perpetuate biases and inequalities. This requires diverse and representative training data, as well as ongoing monitoring to detect and mitigate biases.

Transparency in AI means making the decision-making processes of AI systems understandable to users. Explainable AI (XAI) is crucial for building trust and ensuring that AI systems are used responsibly. Users should be able to understand how AI systems arrive at their decisions and question and challenge these decisions when necessary.

Accountability in AI involves ensuring that there are clear mechanisms for addressing the impacts of AI systems. This includes establishing regulations that hold organizations accountable for the outcomes of their AI systems, particularly in high-stakes applications such as criminal justice, healthcare, and finance.

PREPARING FOR AN AI-DRIVEN FUTURE

As AI continues to shape the future, it is essential to prepare for the opportunities and challenges it presents. Here are some key steps to prepare for an AI-driven future:

- **Embracing Lifelong Learning**

The rapid pace of technological change requires a commitment to lifelong learning. Individuals must continuously update their skills and knowledge to stay relevant in an AI-driven economy. Educational institutions, governments, and businesses should invest in training programs and resources to support continuous learning. This includes developing curricula that incorporate AI and data science and providing opportunities for workers to upskill and reskill throughout their careers.

- **Promoting Ethical AI**

Ensuring that AI technologies are developed and deployed ethically is crucial. This includes addressing biases, ensuring transparency, and promoting accountability. Organizations should establish ethical guidelines and frameworks to guide AI development and use. This involves conducting regular audits of AI systems to detect and address biases, as well as engaging with stakeholders to understand the ethical implications of AI technologies.

- **Fostering Innovation and Collaboration**

Collaboration between governments, industry, academia, and civil society is essential to foster innovation and address the complex challenges posed by AI. Public-private partnerships, research collaborations, and open innovation platforms can drive progress and ensure that AI benefits all members of society. Governments can play a crucial role in supporting AI research and development through funding and policy initiatives, while industry can contribute by sharing knowledge and expertise.

- **Developing Robust Regulatory Frameworks**

Effective regulatory frameworks are necessary to ensure the responsible use of AI while promoting innovation. Policymakers should engage with stakeholders to develop regulations that address the ethical, legal, and social implications of AI technologies. This includes establishing standards for data protection, algorithmic transparency, and accountability and promoting international cooperation to harmonize regulations across borders.

- **Enhancing Public Awareness and Engagement**

Public awareness and engagement are critical to building trust and acceptance of AI technologies. Educating the public about AI, its benefits, and potential risks can help dispel misconceptions and promote informed discussions about its future. This involves creating accessible and transparent communication about AI technologies, as well as involving diverse groups in conversations about the development and use of AI.

WHAT YOU LEARNED

Chapter 11 explored the future of AI by examining emerging trends and technologies, predicting potential impacts, and discussing how to prepare for an AI-driven future. Key trends such as explainable AI, AI and quantum computing, AI for climate change and sustainability, and the convergence of AI and IoT are shaping the future landscape of AI. These advancements promise to enhance the capabilities of AI systems, making them more powerful, efficient, and accessible.

The potential impacts of AI include workforce transformation, healthcare revolution, smart cities, enhanced customer experiences, and ethical and social challenges. AI is set to transform the workforce by creating new job roles while automating routine tasks, requiring continuous learning and upskilling. In healthcare, AI will enhance diagnostics, personalized medicine, and patient care, revolutionizing the field. Smart cities will benefit from the integration of AI and IoT, optimizing infrastructure, transportation, and services for efficiency and sustainability. Enhanced customer experiences will be driven by AI-powered chatbots, virtual assistants, and predictive analytics, transforming industries such as retail and finance.

Preparing for an AI-driven future requires embracing lifelong learning, promoting ethical AI, fostering innovation and collaboration, developing robust regulatory frameworks, and enhancing public awareness and engagement. By understanding these trends and preparing for the future, we can harness AI's potential while ensuring that its benefits are equitably distributed and its challenges are addressed responsibly. This comprehensive approach will help create a future where AI contributes positively to society and improves the quality of life for all.

12

AI RESOURCES & FURTHER LEARNING

BOOKS, COURSES, AND ONLINE RESOURCES

The field of artificial intelligence is vast and ever-evolving, requiring continuous learning to keep up with the latest advancements and methodologies. Numerous books, courses, and online resources are available to help both beginners and seasoned professionals deepen their understanding of AI.

Books

Books are a fundamental resource for learning about AI. They provide comprehensive insights into theories, concepts, and practical applications.

1. "Artificial Intelligence: A Modern Approach" by Stuart Russell and Peter Norvig: Often considered the bible of AI, this book covers a wide range of topics, from basic principles to advanced AI concepts. It is suitable for both beginners and experienced practitioners.

2. "Deep Learning" by Ian Goodfellow, Yoshua Bengio, and Aaron Courville: This book provides an in-depth look at deep learning techniques, which are a subset of machine learning. It covers the mathematical foundations and practical implementation of deep learning models.

3. "Machine Learning Yearning" by Andrew Ng: Written by one of the leading figures in AI, this book offers practical advice on structuring and improving machine learning projects. It is particularly useful for those looking to apply machine learning in real-world scenarios.

4. "Hands-On Machine Learning with Scikit-Learn, Keras, and TensorFlow" by Aurélien Géron: This book provides hands-on examples and exercises to help readers implement machine learning and deep learning models using popular Python libraries.

5. "The Hundred-Page Machine Learning Book" by Andriy Burkov: This concise yet comprehensive book covers essential machine learning concepts and algorithms. It is a great starting point for beginners.

Courses

Online courses offer a structured approach to learning AI, with interactive content and practical assignments.

1. Coursera: Coursera offers a variety of AI and machine learning courses from top universities and institutions. Notable courses include "Machine Learning" by Andrew

Ng from Stanford University and "Deep Learning Specialization" by Andrew Ng, which covers deep learning techniques and applications.

2. edX: edX provides courses from institutions such as MIT and Harvard. The "AI for Everyone" course by Andrew Ng is a popular choice for those looking to understand AI without getting into technical details.

3. Udacity: Udacity offers Nanodegree programs in AI, machine learning, and deep learning. These programs are designed in collaboration with industry leaders and provide hands-on projects to build practical skills.

4. Khan Academy: Khan Academy offers introductory courses in computer science and programming, which are essential foundations for learning AI.

5. DataCamp: DataCamp focuses on data science and analytics, offering courses on machine learning, data manipulation, and statistical analysis.

Online Resources

There are numerous online resources available for learning AI, including tutorials, forums, and research papers.

1. Kaggle: Kaggle is a platform for data science competitions, providing datasets and notebooks for practicing machine learning and AI techniques. It is also a great community for learning from other data scientists.

2. TensorFlow and PyTorch Documentation: The official documentation for TensorFlow and PyTorch provides comprehensive guides and tutorials for using these popular deep learning frameworks.

3. Medium and Towards Data Science: These platforms feature articles and tutorials on various AI topics written by practitioners and researchers in the field.

4. ArXiv: ArXiv is a repository for research papers in AI and machine learning. It is an excellent resource for staying up-to-date with the latest research developments.

5. AI Conferences and Workshops: Attending AI conferences and workshops, such as NeurIPS, ICML, and CVPR, can provide valuable insights into cutting-edge research and industry trends.

Communities and Forums

Engaging with AI communities and forums can significantly enhance the learning experience. These platforms provide opportunities to ask questions, share knowledge, and collaborate with others.

- Online Communities

1. Reddit: Subreddits like r/MachineLearning and r/ArtificialIntelligence are vibrant communities where users discuss AI news, research, and projects.

2. Stack Overflow: Stack Overflow is a go-to platform for

getting help with programming and machine learning problems. The community is active and provides detailed answers to technical questions.

3. GitHub: GitHub is a platform for sharing and collaborating on code. Many AI projects and libraries are hosted on GitHub, making it a valuable resource for learning and contributing to open-source projects.

4. LinkedIn Groups: LinkedIn hosts various groups focused on AI and machine learning, where professionals share insights, job opportunities, and industry trends.

- Meetups and Local Groups

1. Meetup.com: Meetup.com hosts numerous local groups and events focused on AI and machine learning. These meetups provide opportunities to network with other professionals, attend talks, and participate in workshops.

2. Data Science and AI Clubs: Many universities and organizations have data science and AI clubs that organize events, hackathons, and study groups. Joining these clubs can provide hands-on experience and valuable networking opportunities.

- Professional Organizations

1. Association for the Advancement of Artificial Intelligence (AAAI): AAAI is a professional organization dedicated to advancing the understanding of AI. It

organizes conferences and workshops and publishes research in the field.

2. Institute of Electrical and Electronics Engineers (IEEE): IEEE has a dedicated AI and Robotics section that offers resources, conferences, and publications related to AI.

3. Data Science Society: This global community focuses on data science and AI, organizing events, competitions, and providing resources for learning and collaboration.

Staying Updated with the Latest in AI

The field of AI is rapidly evolving, with new research, tools, and techniques emerging regularly. Staying updated with the latest developments is crucial for anyone involved in AI.

- <u>Research Papers and Journals</u>

Reading research papers and journals is essential for staying informed about the latest advancements in AI. Key journals and conferences include:

1. Journal of Artificial Intelligence Research (JAIR): JAIR publishes high-quality research articles covering all aspects of AI.

2. Neural Information Processing Systems (NeurIPS): NeurIPS is one of the most prestigious AI conferences, featuring cutting-edge research in machine learning and neural networks.

3. International Conference on Machine Learning (ICML): ICML is a leading conference for presenting new research in machine learning.

4. IEEE Transactions on Neural Networks and Learning Systems: This journal publishes research on neural networks and learning systems, covering both theoretical and practical aspects.

- <u>Blogs and Newsletters</u>

Subscribing to AI blogs and newsletters can provide regular updates on new developments, tutorials, and industry news.

1. DeepMind Blog: DeepMind's blog features articles on their latest research and breakthroughs in AI.

2. OpenAI Blog: OpenAI shares insights into their research projects and AI advancements.

3. AI Weekly: AI Weekly is a newsletter that curates the latest AI news, research, and articles from around the web.

4. Import AI: Import AI is a weekly newsletter that covers important news and developments in AI, written by Jack Clark.

- <u>Podcasts and Webinars</u>

Listening to AI podcasts and attending webinars can provide insights from experts and keep you updated on the latest trends. Podcasts and webinars are convenient ways to learn on the go and gain diverse perspectives on AI topics.

1. Talking Machines: This podcast features interviews with AI researchers and discussions on current topics in machine learning. It provides insights into both theoretical and practical aspects of AI.

2. The AI Alignment Podcast: Focused on the ethical and philosophical aspects of AI, this podcast explores issues related to AI alignment and safety. It is an excellent resource for understanding the broader implications of AI.

3. Data Skeptic: Data Skeptic covers a wide range of topics in AI and data science, with episodes featuring interviews, tutorials, and discussions. It is suitable for both beginners and experienced practitioners.

4. AI in Business: This podcast focuses on how AI is being applied in various industries, providing practical insights and case studies. It is ideal for professionals looking to understand the impact of AI on business.

- Webinars and Online Conferences

1. AI Summit: The AI Summit is a series of webinars and conferences that bring together industry leaders to discuss the latest trends and applications of AI. Attendees

can learn about cutting-edge research and network with professionals.

2. O'Reilly AI Conference: O'Reilly Media hosts AI conferences that feature talks, tutorials, and hands-on training sessions. These events are an excellent opportunity to learn from experts and gain practical skills.

3. Machine Learning Week: This event includes webinars and conferences focused on machine learning applications in various industries. It provides insights into real-world use cases and best practices.

- Online Communities and Social Media

Engaging with online communities and following AI experts on social media can provide real-time updates and insights. These platforms allow users to stay connected with the AI community and access the latest information.

1. Twitter: Follow AI researchers, practitioners, and organizations on Twitter to stay informed about their latest work and opinions. Hashtags like Machine Learning, Deep Learning, and AI are useful for discovering relevant content. Notable AI influencers and organizations to follow include Andrew Ng, Yann LeCun, and OpenAI.

2. LinkedIn: LinkedIn is a valuable platform for networking with AI professionals and following companies and thought leaders in the field. Joining AI-

related groups and participating in discussions can enhance your knowledge and professional network.

3. Slack Channels: Joining Slack channels dedicated to AI and machine learning, such as AI-specific communities or those hosted by educational platforms, can provide a space for discussion and knowledge sharing. Popular Slack communities include AI and Machine Learning, Data Science Salon, and Kaggle Noobs.

WHAT YOU LEARNED

Chapter 12 explored various resources and avenues for further learning in AI. Books such as "Artificial Intelligence: A Modern Approach" and "Deep Learning" provide comprehensive insights into AI theories and practical applications. Online courses from platforms like Coursera, edX, and Udacity offer structured learning paths and hands-on projects. Online resources, including Kaggle, TensorFlow PyTorch documentation, Medium, and ArXiv, provide valuable tutorials, articles, and research papers.

Engaging with AI communities and forums, such as Reddit, Stack Overflow, GitHub, and LinkedIn groups, enhances the learning experience by allowing users to ask questions, share knowledge, and collaborate. Professional organizations like AAAI and IEEE offer additional resources, conferences, and networking opportunities.

It is crucial to stay updated with the latest developments in AI. This can be achieved by reading research papers and journals, subscribing to AI blogs and newsletters, listening to podcasts, and attending webinars. Engaging with online communities and following AI experts on social media also provides real-time updates and insights.

By leveraging these resources and engaging with the AI community, individuals can continue to learn and stay informed about the rapidly evolving field of artificial intelligence. This comprehensive approach to learning and staying updated will help ensure that AI practitioners and enthusiasts remain at the forefront of AI innovation and application. Continuous learning and active participation in the AI community are essential for staying ahead in this dynamic field.

CONCLUSION

Artificial intelligence (AI) has come a long way since its inception, and its influence spans numerous industries and aspects of daily life. Throughout this book, we have explored various dimensions of AI, from its fundamental principles to its practical applications and future prospects. AI is a branch of computer science focused on creating machines capable of performing tasks that typically require human intelligence, including learning from experience, understanding natural language, recognizing patterns, solving problems, and making decisions. We distinguished between different types of AI, such as narrow AI (designed for specific tasks) and general AI (possessing broad cognitive abilities), and delved into the core concepts of machine learning and deep learning, which are subsets of AI that enable machines to learn from data and improve over time.

The journey of AI has been marked by significant milestones and breakthroughs. From its early beginnings in the 1950s, with pioneers like Alan Turing and John McCarthy laying the groundwork, to the development of expert systems in the 1980s and the rise of machine learning in the 2000s, AI has evolved through various phases of innovation and setbacks. The evolution of AI has been driven by advancements in computing power, the availability of large datasets, and the development of sophisticated algorithms. Key moments, such as the defeat of world chess champion Garry Kasparov by IBM's Deep Blue and the more recent victory of Google's AlphaGo over Go champion Lee Sedol, highlight the rapid progress of AI capabilities.

Understanding AI requires familiarity with its core concepts and terminology. Algorithms and models are the building blocks of AI systems. Data is the fuel that powers AI, and the quality and preprocessing of this data are crucial for building and evaluating AI models. Training, testing, and validation are essential steps in developing AI models, ensuring they learn patterns from data and generalize well to new data. AI has transformative applications across various industries, enhancing diagnostics, personalized medicine, and patient care in healthcare, improving fraud detection, algorithmic trading, and risk management in finance, and driving predictive maintenance, quality control, and supply chain optimization in manufacturing. Self-driving cars leverage

AI to navigate and make driving decisions, promising safer and more efficient transportation.

The rapid adoption of AI brings ethical and societal challenges. Privacy concerns arise from the vast amounts of data collected by AI systems, necessitating robust data security measures and informed consent from individuals. Bias and fairness in AI are significant issues, as biased algorithms can lead to discriminatory outcomes. The impact of AI on the workforce is another area of concern, as it can both create new job roles and pose the risk of job displacement. Addressing these challenges requires ethical AI development practices, continuous learning, and investment in education and training.

Looking ahead, AI is poised to continue its transformative impact. Emerging trends such as explainable AI (XAI), AI and quantum computing, and AI for climate change and sustainability promise to enhance AI capabilities and address global challenges. The convergence of AI and the Internet of Things (IoT) is creating intelligent, interconnected systems that improve efficiency and convenience in various domains. Ensuring ethical and responsible AI development remains paramount, with collaborative efforts between governments, industry, academia, and civil society essential for establishing ethical guidelines and regulatory frameworks.

As we conclude this comprehensive guide to artificial intelligence, it is important to reflect on the immense potential and responsibility that comes with the development and deployment of AI technologies. AI has the power to revolutionize industries, enhance human capabilities, and address some of the most pressing challenges of our time. However, this potential must be harnessed responsibly, with a commitment to ethical principles and societal well-being. Embracing the potential of AI involves recognizing the unprecedented opportunities it offers to improve our lives and solve complex problems, from advancing healthcare to creating more efficient transportation systems.

The development and deployment of AI technologies must be guided by ethical considerations, ensuring that AI systems are fair, transparent, and accountable. This involves addressing biases, protecting privacy, and making decisions that benefit society as a whole. Continuous learning and adaptation are essential in the dynamic and rapidly evolving field of AI. Lifelong learning through books, courses, and online resources is critical for maintaining expertise and adapting to new developments. Engaging with AI communities and forums provides opportunities for collaboration, knowledge sharing, and staying updated on industry trends.

To those who are just beginning their journey in AI, remember that this field is vast and full of opportunities for innovation and discovery. The learning curve may seem steep, but with dedication and curiosity, you can develop the skills and knowledge needed to make meaningful contributions. AI is a multidisciplinary field, and diverse perspectives and expertise are essential for driving progress. Experienced practitioners continue pushing the boundaries of what is possible with AI. Your work has the potential to shape the future and create technologies that benefit humanity. Stay committed to ethical practices, engage with the broader AI community, and mentor the next generation of AI professionals.

In this book, we have explored the multifaceted world of artificial intelligence, from its foundational principles to its practical applications and future prospects. AI has the potential to revolutionize industries, enhance human capabilities, and address global challenges. However, harnessing this potential responsibly requires a commitment to ethical principles, continuous learning, and proactive adaptation to new developments. By understanding these trends and preparing for the future, we can harness the potential of AI while ensuring that its benefits are equitably distributed and its challenges are addressed responsibly. This comprehensive approach will help create a future where AI contributes positively to society and improves the quality of life for all.

Thank You for Reading!

Congratulations on completing *Understanding Artificial Intelligence {AI}*! I hope this journey into the world of AI has been as enlightening and inspiring for you as it was for me to create.

SCAN TO REVIEW BOOK

If you found value in this book, I'd be grateful if you could take a moment to leave a review on Amazon. Your feedback helps others discover the book and ensures future readers can benefit from your insights.

Thank you for your time, your support, and for being part of this incredible series. I hope we meet again in ***Volume Two***, *"From Algorithms to Art: How AI is Shaping the Creative World."*

ADDITIONAL READING & RESOURCES

Books:

1. "The Master Algorithm" by Pedro Domingos: An exploration of the quest for the ultimate learning algorithm that can solve any problem.

2. "Human Compatible: Artificial Intelligence and the Problem of Control" by Stuart Russell: A look at the potential risks of AI and how we can ensure it aligns with human values.

Online Courses:

1. "Machine Learning" by Andrew Ng on Coursera: An introductory course covering the basics of machine learning.

2. "Deep Learning Specialization" by Andrew Ng on

Coursera: A series of courses focusing on deep learning techniques.

3. "AI For Everyone" by Andrew Ng on Coursera: A non-technical course designed to help everyone understand AI and its applications.

4. "Introduction to TensorFlow for Artificial Intelligence, Machine Learning, and Deep Learning" on Coursera: A practical course on using TensorFlow for AI projects.

5. "Data Science and Machine Learning Bootcamp with R" on Udemy: A comprehensive course on data science and machine learning using R programming.

Websites and Blogs:

1. Towards Data Science: A Medium publication sharing concepts, ideas, and codes on data science and AI.

2. Kaggle: A platform for data science competitions that also offers datasets and educational resources.

3. ArXiv: A repository of research papers in various fields, including AI and machine learning.

4. OpenAI Blog: Articles and research updates from OpenAI, a leading AI research organization.

5. DeepMind Blog: Insights and updates from DeepMind, a pioneer in AI research.

Communities and Forums:

1. Reddit (r/MachineLearning, r/ArtificialIntelligence): Active communities discussing the latest in AI and machine learning.

2. Stack Overflow: A question-and-answer site for programming and coding, including AI-related queries.

3. GitHub: A platform for sharing and collaborating on code with numerous AI projects and repositories.

4. LinkedIn Groups: Professional groups focused on AI and machine learning, useful for networking and knowledge sharing.

5. Meetup.com: Local groups and events for AI and machine learning enthusiasts.

APPENDIX

GLOSSARY OF AI TERMS

Algorithm: A set of rules or instructions given to an AI designed to solve problems or perform specific tasks.

Artificial Intelligence (AI): The simulation of human intelligence processes by machines, especially computer systems. This includes learning (acquiring information and rules for using it), reasoning (using rules to reach approximate or definite conclusions), and self-correction.

Big Data: Extremely large datasets that may be analyzed computationally to reveal patterns, trends, and associations, especially relating to human behavior and interactions.

Bias: In AI, bias refers to systematic and unfair discrimination in algorithms or data, often resulting in prejudiced outcomes.

Classification: The process of predicting the class or category of a given data point from among predefined classes.

Clustering: Grouping a set of objects in such a way that objects in the same group (cluster) are more similar to each other than to those in other groups.

Computer Vision: A field of AI that trains computers to interpret and understand the visual world, including recognizing and processing images and videos.

Data Mining: The practice of examining large pre-existing databases to generate new information and find hidden patterns.

Deep Learning: A subset of machine learning involving neural networks with many layers used for high-level data abstraction.

Feature Extraction: The process of transforming raw data into a set of features that can be used in machine learning models.

General AI: Hypothetical AI that exhibits human-like cognitive abilities across a wide range of tasks.

Machine Learning: A subset of AI that involves the use of algorithms and statistical models to enable computers to improve their performance on a task with experience.

Natural Language Processing (NLP): The ability of a computer program to understand, process, and generate human language.

Neural Network: A series of algorithms that attempt to recognize underlying relationships in a set of data through a process that mimics the way the human brain operates.

Overfitting: A modeling error that occurs when a machine learning algorithm models the training data too well, capturing noise and details that negatively impact its performance on new data.

Reinforcement Learning: A type of machine learning where an agent learns to make decisions by performing certain actions and receiving rewards or penalties.

Supervised Learning: A type of machine learning where the model is trained on labeled data, meaning that each training example is paired with an output label.

Training Data: The dataset used to train an AI model, typically consisting of inputs and corresponding outputs.

Unsupervised Learning: A type of machine learning where the model is trained on data that does not have labeled responses, aiming to infer the natural structure present within a set of data points.

Validation Data: A set of data used to provide an

unbiased evaluation of a model fit during the training phase.

Weights: Parameters within a neural network that are adjusted during training to minimize error in the output.

Zero-shot Learning: The ability of a machine learning model to correctly make predictions about unseen classes without any labeled training data for those classes.

ABOUT US

Books of Understanding

Produced by J.F. Graley

Welcome to the world of Books of Understanding, conceived by the visionary J.F. Graley. Prepare to embark on an exhilarating journey through a curated collection spanning diverse topics. From the cutting-edge domain of Computers & Technology to the enriching realms of Health & Wellness, from the thought-provoking corridors of Politics & Social Sciences to the tender intricacies of Parenting & Relationships, our books are your gateway to a world of knowledge and discovery. The ever-growing list of topical categories is as follows:

- Computer & Technology
- Health & Wellness
- Politics & Social Sciences
- Environmental Sciences
- Human History
- Parenting & Relationships
- Religion & Spirituality, and

- Adventure Travel

But here's the twist: we're not just offering books but igniting a passion for learning. Each meticulously chosen volume is designed to captivate, inspire, and empower readers like you to explore, learn, and grow.

Imagine peering into the latest technological innovations, embracing a healthier lifestyle, or gaining fresh perspectives on pressing societal issues—all within the captivating pages of our collection.

So, are you ready to embark on an odyssey of enlightenment? Join us as we delve into knowledge with Books of Understanding.

Let curiosity be your compass, and let our books be your guide to a world of endless discovery. Your next adventure awaits— start exploring what's next.

Thank you for your support.

WHAT'S NEXT

Step into the future of creativity with "Understanding Artificial Intelligence {AI} Volume Two

From Algorithms to Art: *How AI is Shaping the Creative World.*"

This book is your passport to the cutting-edge world where artificial intelligence meets artistic genius, offering a vivid exploration of how AI is revolutionizing music, visual arts, literature, performance art, and beyond.

SCAN ME

This comprehensive guide explores the dynamic intersection of artificial intelligence and artistic expression, offering readers an in-depth look at how AI is revolutionizing music, visual arts, literature, performance art, and more.

What Awaits You Inside:

- Innovative Technologies: Discover the latest AI advancements reshaping the creative landscape, from generative design and deep learning to natural language processing and AI-driven music composition.
- Real-World Marvels: Immerse yourself in fascinating case studies and real-life examples showcasing how artists and technologists collaborate to push the boundaries of creativity.
- Ethical Explorations: Delve into the ethical and philosophical dilemmas of AI-generated art, addressing questions of authorship, ownership, and fairness.
- Future Gazing: Peek into the emerging technologies and trends poised to define the future of AI in the arts.
- Practical Playbook: Gain actionable tips and strategies to seamlessly integrate AI into your creative toolkit, whether you're an artist, musician, writer, or tech innovator.

Join the revolution of forward-thinking creatives and tech visionaries shaping the future of art and innovation. Don't let this opportunity slip away—dive into the limitless world of AI-enhanced creativity and transform your artistic vision today!

introduced us to the concept of seven distinct stages in the life cycle of great nations.

- Stage 1: The Age of Pioneers (Outburst)
- Stage 2: The Age of Conquest
- Stage 3: The Age of Commerce (Invention, Infrastructure, Industry)
- Stage 4: The Age of Affluence (Economic Gain)
- Stage 5: The Age of Intellect (Enlightenment)
- Stage 6: The Age of Decadence (Degeneration)
- Stage 7: The Age of Decline and Collapse

Our focus lies within Stage 6, The Age of Decadence. This stage is marked by moral and societal decay, where once-held values are eroded, and the seeds of decline are sown.

Through meticulous research and thoughtful analysis, the book examines the indicators of decadence, including moral decay, societal degeneration, and the erosion of values. It explores the role of religion, education, and cultural movements in shaping American identity and highlights the challenges posed by economic and geopolitical shifts.

Drawing parallels with past empires, the book offers valuable insights into the consequences of societal decline and the potential paths forward for the nation. Written with clarity and insight, "The Death of America" prompts readers to reflect on the complex issues facing contemporary society and encourages a deeper understanding of the forces driving its decline. Engaging and thought-provoking, this book is essential reading for anyone seeking to comprehend the challenges confronting the United States in the 21st century.

Prepare to delve into the labyrinth of atheism's historical roots, where ancient philosophers dared to question the divine and pave the way for a modern renaissance of skepticism. From the fiery debates of Enlightenment thinkers to the contemporary discourse of secular humanists, the journey unfolds, revealing the evolution of atheism as a powerful force in shaping the trajectory of human thought.

But our exploration doesn't stop there. We journey deep into the philosophical depths of atheism, where logical arguments clash, existential inquiries linger, and alternative explanations for the universe beckon. Here, we confront the age-old dilemma of the problem of evil, ponder the mysteries of existence, and confront the boundaries of human knowledge in the quest for truth.

As our journey continues, we navigate the labyrinthine corridors of atheism's psychological landscape, where cognitive patterns intertwine, personality traits emerge, and the human psyche grapples with the absence of the divine.

But atheism is more than just a philosophical stance; it is a social force that reverberates through the corridors of power, shapes the contours of morality, and challenges the fabric of society. In the crucible of social discourse, atheists stand as beacons of reason, advocates for secularism, and champions of human rights, as they navigate the complex terrain of religious pluralism and cultural diversity.

Whether you're a curious skeptic, a devout believer, or intrigued by intellectual discourse, this thought-provoking book offers a compelling invitation to explore the diversity of human beliefs and the quest for truth in an ever-changing world.

SOURCES:

List of Sources used in the creation of this book.

Books:

"Artificial Intelligence: A Modern Approach" by Stuart Russell and Peter Norvig: Comprehensive insights on AI concepts and methodologies.

"Deep Learning" by Ian Goodfellow, Yoshua Bengio, and Aaron Courville: Detailed explanation of deep learning techniques.

"Hands-On Machine Learning with Scikit-Learn, Keras, and TensorFlow" by Aurélien Géron: Practical guide on implementing machine learning models.

"The Hundred-Page Machine Learning Book" by Andriy

Burkov: Concise overview of essential machine learning concepts.

"Machine Learning Yearning" by Andrew Ng: Practical advice on structuring machine learning projects.

Online Courses:

Coursera: "Machine Learning" by Andrew Ng, "Deep Learning Specialization" by Andrew Ng.

edX: "AI for Everyone" by Andrew Ng.

Udacity: Nanodegree programs in AI, machine learning, and deep learning.

Khan Academy: Introductory courses in computer science and programming.

DataCamp: Courses on machine learning, data manipulation, and statistical analysis.

Websites and Blogs:

Towards Data Science: Medium publication sharing concepts, ideas, and codes on data science and AI.

Kaggle: Platform for data science competitions, datasets, and educational resources.

ArXiv: Repository of research papers in AI and machine learning.

OpenAI Blog: Articles and research updates from OpenAI.

DeepMind Blog: Insights and updates from DeepMind.

Communities and Forums:

Reddit: r/MachineLearning, r/ArtificialIntelligence.

Stack Overflow: Programming and coding Q&A site.

GitHub: Platform for sharing and collaborating on code.

LinkedIn Groups: Professional groups focused on AI and machine learning.

Meetup.com: Local groups and events for AI and machine learning enthusiasts.

Podcasts and Webinars:

Talking Machines: Interviews with AI researchers and discussions on current topics.

The AI Alignment Podcast: Focus on ethical and philosophical aspects of AI.

Data Skeptic: Covers a wide range of topics in AI and data science.

AI in Business: Practical insights on how AI is applied in various industries.

AI Summit, O'Reilly AI Conference, Machine Learning

Week: Webinars and online conferences featuring industry leaders and experts.

Research Papers and Journals:

Journal of Artificial Intelligence Research (JAIR): High-quality research articles on AI.

Neural Information Processing Systems (NeurIPS): Prestigious AI conference.

International Conference on Machine Learning (ICML): Leading conference for machine learning research.

IEEE Transactions on Neural Networks and Learning Systems: Research on neural networks and learning systems.

Professional Organizations:

Association for the Advancement of Artificial Intelligence (AAAI): Resources, conferences, and research publications.

Institute of Electrical and Electronics Engineers (IEEE): The AI and Robotics section offers resources and events.

Data Science Society: Global community organizing events and providing resources for data science and AI.

Printed in Great Britain
by Amazon

56379394R00145